The *Ultimate* Youth Drama Book

Everything you need!
(Except stage, cast, audience etc.)

Paul McCusker

MONARCH
BOOKS

Mill Hill, London NW7 3SA and Grand Rapids, Michigan 49501

First published by Gazelle Books in the UK in 2000.
Reissued in 2001 by Monarch Books, Concorde House,
Grenville Place, Mill Hill, London NW7 3SA.

Published in the USA by Monarch Books 2001.

Distributed by:
UK: STL, PO Box 300, Kingstown Broadway, Carlisle
Cumbria CA3 0QS;
USA: Kregel Publications, PO Box 2607
Grand Rapids, Michigan 49501.

ISBN 1 85424 546 5 (UK)
ISBN 0 8254 6003 4 (USA)

British Library Cataloguing Data
A catalogue record for this book is available
from the British Library.

Designed and produced for the publishers by:
Gazelle Creative Productions Ltd, Concorde House,
Grenville Place, Mill Hill, London NW7 3SA.

Printed and bound in Great Britain by Biddles Ltd, *www.biddles.co.uk*

For Chuck Bolte,
Without whom this book wouldn't have been possible.
(The cheque's in the post.)

Contents

Sketches for the more adventurous

Introduction: Why this book can help your group (and you)

One of two things has happened to make you pick up this book.

You have a burning passion, a deep stirring, a *calling* to do dramas for your youth club, your church, your school, or perhaps for some other group.

Or you've been 'volunteered' by someone who thought doing drama would be a good idea.

I'm happy to report that, either way, this book should be helpful to you. Pushing past all the pretence and technical verbiage and preconceived notions about drama, I hope to present a fun, 'hands-on' approach to putting on sketches for your youth club, church or organisation. This is going to be a book you should be able to *use* – with mangled, dog-eared pages – and not just one of those that sits on your shelf with the other books that you gave up as being unrealistic. This is a roll-up-your-sleeves-and-dig-in kind of book.

And it doesn't matter whether you have a lot of experience or only a little. The truth is: I didn't have any formal training when I started writing and directing dramas at my church. It was enough to simply *do it* and learn along the way. Hopefully, this book will give you the means to give it your best try.

How drama can help your group
It's easy to assume that because we have a long, diverse and rich tradition of drama it's understood *why* drama is worthwhile. Briefly, here are a few reasons:

- Drama is a unique way to get across familiar stories or points of view in an unfamiliar way. Nothing turns a Bible story or moral lesson on its head like a dramatic re-telling.
- Drama turns abstract ideas into human realities. Discussions are no longer vague once you have a flesh-and-blood character playing out a particular conflict or clash of ideals.
- Drama allows the members of your group to stretch beyond themselves, trying things they've never tried before. You'll be pleasantly surprised at the new interest and unity born out of drama productions.
- Drama can build your members' confidence and self-esteem. (They'll receive positive attention for doing positive things.)
- Drama can give young people unforgettable experiences.
- Drama can create an environment of teamwork and cohesiveness.
- Drama provides ways for young people to discover, expand and use their creative abilities.

What will this book do for me?
Part One of this book will cover the wide variety of topics you'll need to know about to produce drama in your youth group. For example:

- How to decide what type of production is best for your specific situation.
- How to determine goals and a budget (a *what?*).
- How to audition your youth members for parts.
- How to run rehearsals.
- How to direct the production from beginning to end.
- How to understand acting terms, like Stage Right, Stage Left, Blocking, etc.
- How to work with props, sets, make-up, costumes, lighting and sound.

Part Two includes scripts that cover topics related to going out, parents, faith, sex, spirituality, church, love, reconciliation... a real Lancashire hot-pot of material. Ideally, you may be able to use them for:

- Discussion starters for virtually any sort of gathering.
- Teaching supplements for worship and special services or classes.
- Puppets, street ministries, coffee-houses, or other forms of outreach.
- Just for the fun of it.

Use your imagination and feel free to adapt them to your particular situation if you need to.

And, as a matter of convenience, the price of this book allows you to make as many copies of the scripts as you need for your immediate group.

A philosophical note
Your biggest battles with drama will involve *balances*. You'll have to balance the message against the medium (or good theatrical technique), goals against guesswork, purpose against performance, your desire to be expressive against your audience's expectations, creativity against communication.

Certain people will argue, various artists will disagree, and you may find yourself rethinking certain assumptions you've had, but I believe that the most satisfying production will be the one that keeps the scales right in the centre, achieving the best on all sides.

Balance. It's all a matter of balance.

With that said, I think we should begin.

Please, step this way...

Part One

Chapter One: Why bother with drama anyway?

Every book has to start somewhere and this one may as well start at the beginning. Not the beginning of drama, as such, but some perspectives about it that might help you convince the sceptics around you that to produce drama isn't merely a whim on your part. For centuries, Drama has had a significant place in the larger, Scriptural, and historical picture of Life.

Purists beware: I won't be taking a conventional route to justify that statement.

A biblical base for drama

I won't kid you on this. If you're looking for a direct scripture verse saying something like, 'And he went among his kindred, performing drama to the glorification of the Lord, and the blessings of the multitudes were upon him' (1 Pontifications 2:3), forget it. Such a verse doesn't exist. But that doesn't mean drama is somehow *un*scriptural. All you have to do is look through the Bible and you'll see that it's full of drama. Have you read the book of Esther recently? Or how about Job? Or the account of the rise and fall of Saul and David? All of the elements of drama can be found there in the humanity, failures, ironic twists, victories, betrayals, love, bitterness and celebrations. *Home and Away* has nothing on the Bible when it comes to being a good soap opera. It's no wonder the Bible is constantly being adapted for stage and screen – through literal adaptation, allusion, symbolic reference, or blatant plagiarism. It's perfect for them.

Drama and its use in the church

Considering that drama was a mainstay of the church for centuries, it's hard to say why it seems like most churches struggle with it now. Perhaps it simply isn't thought about much. Or perhaps it's considered unsophisticated and childish – like an old toy one has a fondness for but wouldn't dare bring out in public. Perhaps it's like an untidy room and people don't know where to *start* to get it organised. Or perhaps it's one of those art forms that slipped its tether and drifted across the bay to some other shore, where it is now beached – or dry-docked – or sinking (depending on how you feel about the current state of theatre in your country). I could regale you with more word pictures, but won't. Thank God.

It's possible that church leaders steer clear of drama because of its potential to irritate. It's like music. There are numerous forms and styles and, whatever you try to do with it, you're going to step on somebody's taste-buds (or their artistic toes).

This is a valid reaction. At its best drama is an exploration of human issues as seen through character, action and conflict. It may not always come to conclusions about human issues, but it should certainly ask the right questions. The fact that it *doesn't* answer all the questions about life is irksome to some people in the church who want drama to be a public relations campaign for God, Jesus Christ and Christianity.

Don't get me wrong. Drama can certainly communicate a message or truth. In fact, it *should*. But that message or truth must be borne out realistically

through the character, action and conflict. Not the
other way around.

On the other hand, there have been plenty of plays
performed in churches that were so vague and obscure
– so inaccessibly *theatrical* in the worst sense – that
church leaders viewed any further productions with
wary and sceptical eyes.

Where does that leave you as the leader of drama?
Well, the main consideration for using drama in the
church is this: *what is most appropriate for your audience?*
Should it be a straight drama or a tragedy or allegory or
melodrama or fantasy? What style should be used:
something realistic or abstract or impressionistic or
romantic?

The key is to be sensitive to what will work for your
particular audience. Yes, you can be creative and
experimental and, of course, you don't want to insult
their intelligence, but you must always balance your
artistic vision with what is appropriate for your
audience.

There's another reason that some people want to
steer clear of drama. It's often done so poorly. How
often have we heard it said that the problem with
typical church dramas are just that: they're *typical
church dramas*. It's as if somebody somewhere decided
that to be considered church drama, it must be second-
rate, over-written and over-acted to become a blunt
instrument with which to beat an audience senseless.

Hopefully, we can prove them all wrong.

Humour and comedy

Though I use 'drama' as a catch-all phrase, I believe it's
worth talking about humour and comedy as separate
items for just a moment.

First to clarify terms: humour is an attitude, a

disposition. Comedy is a theatrical term that utilises humour. They're related but distinct.

At face value, humour is proven to be a vital part of our human existence. Practical experience shows that good humour is healthy, it relieves tension, creates better circulation, literally heals certain physical ailments, and might even be a cure for Mad Cow Disease.

Humour and its theatrical form, comedy, breaks down communication barriers. The most skilful communicators, writers, politicians, salesmen and ministers know to use humour and comedy to make the listener more receptive to their message or idea. The effective use of humour and comedy creates an atmosphere of openness designed to disarm the listener.

Consider the humour found in the Bible. Granted, it's not the same type of one-liners or wit we're used to today, but you will find humour. Solomon, for all of the moroseness of Ecclesiastes, turns around in Proverbs with his tongue firmly implanted in his cheek – or wisdom-tooth – and presents a very ironic look at the state of man and his world. Proverbs 27:15–16 from the *New Living Translation*: 'A nagging wife is as annoying as the constant dripping on a rainy day. Trying to stop her complaints is like trying to stop the wind or hold something with greased hands.' Or Proverbs 26:14: 'As a door turns back and forth on its hinges, so the lazy person turns over in bed.'

Not only do the phrases make for good humour, but they're perfect as Jewish fortune-cookies. (And, yes, I know that this example is correct only if you allow that Solomon wrote all of Ecclesiastes and Proverbs. If he didn't, it was probably because of all his wives and concubines.)

While we may not think of Jesus as a stand-up

comedian, we have to admit that he knew the value of a good turn of phrase or an absurd image. Picture the expression where he tells his listeners to take the logs out of their own eyes before they try to take the speck out of someone else's.

Not that the disciples were rolling on the ground doubled up with laughter – they probably weren't. The Pharisees *certainly* weren't. But it's a good example of Jesus' use of absurdist humour – the humour of exaggeration.

'Straining a gnat and swallowing a camel', or getting a camel through 'the eye of a needle', are other examples.

But what's the role of comedy within youth groups? Apart from the obvious slapstick belly laughs and the toilet humour we so often see on television, where is its value? One could argue that laughter in and of itself is enough. Comedy can be extremely useful for youth 'ice-breakers' and just for fun at different activities.

Yet I think we look to our churches to provide humour that goes beyond just laughter as an end unto itself. We hope after the laughter has died down that something has touched our minds and hearts. Through the comedy we have seen the quirks and foibles of our humanity, religiosity, and society through irony, absurdity, farce and satire. We haven't laughed out of emptiness, but out of the recognition of ourselves.

To sum it up in a word, we look to our churches to give us humour that is *redemptive*. This is the most distinctive characteristic of comedy and drama from a Christian perspective.

The bottom line

In our art, *Redemption* says it's not enough to wallow in the mud with everyone else; we must communicate *hope* of a transformed life. Like Christ and through

Christ, we must 'come down' in our artistic forms to meet people where they are, and then 'rise up' again – helping them and us to get out of the complacency, the despair, the hopelessness, the unredemptive, and the suffering.

Drama can do it. Drama can have a significant impact in our emotional, physical, social and spiritual lives. One way or another, through television, films, radio, and stage, we're being influenced and affected. We can easily forget a sermon or lecture, but we don't quickly forget an effective drama.

For proof, you need only think of the last play you went to – and then go to another. Or watch *Home and Away* or any popular soap opera. Why do you think so many people are hooked on them?

My father-in-law, who is more a mathematician than artist, once tossed off this gem to me. 'Drama needs to make us forget about our lives – or give us insight into them.' The very best dramas do one or the other.

Which would you like to do?

Chapter Two: What sort of drama and ... who pays?

Before I wrote a single word for this book, I had to sit down and hammer out a 'statement of purpose' for what this book was to be. I considered who I was writing to, what I should put in it, the kind of style it should have, the format, and two or three other ideals that I then tried to articulate in one or two sentences. That done, I sent it to my editor and, with his input, I clarified my goals even more. From there, I put together a general outline of each chapter and, once that was approved, began the actual writing.

Had I skipped those early procedures, I might have saved time and had a book on the market sooner but there's no telling what the book would have been like. All things considered, it could have started off dealing with drama and wandered into a discussion of improving your golf swing, 101 uses for belly-button lint, or getting rid of fungus in the garden.

The point is: anything of reasonable importance must be the result of specific goals and proper planning.

In other words, before you try to do any drama, you'd better have a good idea of what you're trying to accomplish. Otherwise, your good idea could become a Frankenstein's monster – killing the maker, destroying the village and creating a whole series of terrible films (aka: draining you and your church of your time, energy, and resources).

If you're doing a one-off production, ask yourself these questions:

1. What is its purpose?
2. What would you like to see within the cast and production crew – spiritually, emotionally?
3. What are you trying to accomplish with your audience?
4. When the final curtain has dropped, what was the point of the whole thing?

If you're trying to start a drama group, add these questions:

1. What is the purpose of the group?
2. Will they do productions for the church?
3. What kind of productions: full-length plays, musicals, dinner theatre, one-acts?
4. How many productions will it do in a year?
5. If not full productions, will they simply do short sketches for various services or activities?
6. Is it a group that you might want to take 'on the road'?
7. Or maybe you just want a group for 'workshop' purposes to help cultivate acting abilities, creative talent, or simply provide an alternative to those who have nothing better to do with their time.
8. Or maybe it will be all of the above?

The answers to these questions and more must be considered before you get started (a more detailed list of questions can be found at the end of this chapter).

If you *don't* answer these questions at the beginning, you'll find yourself frustrated, your group will be confused, your church leaders will question your salvation, and your congregation will ask you to return the key to the vestry.

None of this is to say that your early goals and planning can't be modified as you progress. They can. You'll find several unexpected twists and turns in the direction your production or group takes. You'll need to be flexible. But no matter what comes your way, you will have the initial foundation of goals established and there to fall back upon.

This isn't the West End

Be realistic with your goals. This isn't the West End. Too often a church or organisation decides to start a drama group, throw everything they have into an extravagant production, and then if it flops, believe that it was God's way of telling them never to do drama again.

If you're just beginning, start small and see how it grows. Give yourself room to learn, to adapt, to make mistakes. Start by using short sketches in a variety of situations (services, activities, etc.). If that goes well, then put together a variety show with short sketches and music. From there, try a one-act play. Then possibly a full-length play. Then maybe a musical and/or a dinner theatre. And from there... anything can happen.

But *whatever* you do, don't jump too far ahead of yourself (or your church) with grandiose visions of elaborate costumes, intricate lights and sound, or enormous sets. Chances are it'll backfire on you in a number of horrible-too-gruesome-to-describe ways. Here are a couple of reasons why...

The desire and the dosh

After you have it fixed in your mind what your goals are and you want to get some degree of church (or organisational) approval, one question will certainly raise its ugly head. Yes, beyond your vision, beyond the benefits for everyone everywhere, and beyond the larger, scriptural, and historical scheme of eternity, someone is going to ask... What will it cost us?

Cost? You ask, incredulously. *You must be joking. We don't have any money.*

If this is the case, then you may quickly move past this section.

On the other hand, if you do have access to a few pounds, then carry on.

If you've done your planning properly, you'll be able to smile confidently and explain that it won't cost much to do short sketches with two chairs representing a front room and regular clothes serving as your costumes and the technical facilities in the church serving perfectly as your stage, sound and lights. And you'll sound very sane. And you'll sound very reasonable. And maybe you'll get the money you need for those incidental items that inevitably come along.

The other scenario would be a long list of material, sets, lights, microphones, electricity, facilities, and time you'll need to put together something like a Cecil B. DeMille film. They might go for it through your powers of persuasion or their own personal visions. But if it bombs... don't say I didn't warn you.

Be realistic. Most churches don't look too kindly on what appears to be wasted money.

As you put together your goals and budget, keep in mind a few things:

1. Work *with* your church leadership. Don't take an adversarial role even if you run up against sceptics and resistance. Maintain a spirit of co-operation.
2. Expect that your drama production or group will have to prove itself. From the very first minute of its existence, you'll have to establish credibility with your leadership, congregation and even those in your group. This isn't true only in the area of money but in the types of productions you do (choice of scripts, content, topics, and other things I'll explore in later chapters). Every step of the way, you'll be working to legitimise what you're doing so that everyone will see that it's not just an artistic whim, an extravagant idea or a self-indulgent scheme.
3. Remember that not everyone will be as dedicated or as involved as you are. There will be times you'll want to rehearse and three of your cast members have a football match, or the room you need to rehearse in has been re-scheduled for someone else's meeting, or... well, you get the idea.

You may be wondering, then: if you have consistent successes, will you have full co-operation from your PCC and credibility with your detractors? Maybe, maybe not. Never what you think you deserve, in any event.

But don't be quick to pull the creative wagons in a circle or encourage an 'us-against-them, they-just-don't-understand-art' mentality. Remember point No. 1 and work hard and diplomatically to get the support you need. Then if you constantly run up against opposition, you should either double-check what you're doing or realise that your church isn't ready for this sort of ministry.

This is all well and good, but I still don't know where to start...

Here are areas to ponder while you're setting your goals and establishing your budget.

1. What is the purpose of this specific production/the overall group?
2. Who is our audience – our own congregation, other Christians, general community?
3. Will our production/group work through the church or will our primary focus be external ('on the road'/evangelistic in nature)?
4. Will we perform in the church or at another site? Will we have to pay a rental fee? Will someone set up the auditorium (seats, etc) for us or will we have to do it ourselves? Who will tidy up after the performance is over?
5. When and how often will we perform?
6. Where will we rehearse and how often?
7. What will we perform? Will our script be original or will we use something published? If published, how much will it cost to buy or rent the appropriate number of copies? Will there be performance fees involved?
8. Who will direct?
9. Will we cast strictly from within the church or open it up for outsiders to participate?
10. What kind of technical assistance do we need? Who will head up costumes? Lights? Sound? Sets? Multi-media? What do we need in addition to what's available and how much will it cost to buy or rent?
11. What about music? Do I want to incorporate any? If so, will it be performed live or on tape? Is it copyrighted and will I have to pay any sort of fees to perform it?

12. What kind of publicity do we want – press releases, posters, flyers? Who will be in charge of writing and distributing them?

13. Based on our church beliefs, should we charge admission or take an offering? In either case, do we need to distribute tickets? If so, who will be in charge of that? Should we distribute them through various ticket outlets? Through the mail? By phone? At the door? How much should we charge for the tickets?

14. Will there be child care the night of the performance(s)? Ushers?

15. What kinds of 'miscellaneous' expenditures do we anticipate? Be scrupulous, this is a category that'll sneak up on you during the production.

16. As you're putting together your budget, avoid guessing at expenses that you don't really know about. Take the time to find out from someone who *knows*. Make a few phone calls to be sure of prices.

Once you get rolling, you'll think of more than these since every church, organisation or venue has its own unique set of circumstances. But don't let it intimidate you. Many of these questions will get answered in a 'domino' fashion (as you answer one question, it'll fall into the next and get answered as well). Don't get lazy either. Better to ask all of these questions before you start than find yourself struggling with them in the middle – when it's too late to deal with them correctly.

Now let's roll up our sleeves and dig into some of the details about doing drama.

Chapter Three: Finding scripts, writing scripts

Go to your friendly neighbourhood bookstore, move past the wall of better-way-to-do-it best-sellers, the latest fiction from the top three best-selling authors, the cards for all occasions, the badges, key rings, and book marks, and you may happen upon a pleasant individual who will ask if she can help you in some way. You'll nod and say, 'Do you have any books of drama for use in the church or schools?'

The pleasant individual will look at you quizzically, 'I beg your pardon?'

'You know, skits and plays? Performed on a stage?'

The pleasant individual scratches a chin, shrugs, and says, 'I don't think we carry anything like that but I'll show you what we have.'

And in some dusty corner you may find a leftover from some ancient children's drama book (copyrighted 1954) that wasn't popular then and certainly isn't useable now.

A little background

A lot of people complain that they want to do drama but can't find material to perform. A lot of the publishers complain that they *want to* publish drama for churches and schools but won't because it doesn't sell.

Who's right?

Sadly, both sides are. Publishers need to make money to survive and publishing drama isn't a terribly lucrative way to do that.

But it's not all doom and gloom. The advent of the Internet gives the would-be drama producer plenty of places to look for material. Some of it may be pretty good. Some, unfortunately, will be exactly what you've come to expect. It's going to be hit-and-miss no matter what you do. But knowing *what* to look for will help limit the amount of wasted time.

Let's talk about that.

What to look for

Even before you begin your search for material, you must have some idea of what you're looking for. Your group is unique – with specific needs and goals – and whatever you do needs to reflect such things. As I've mentioned elsewhere, you have to be aware of your audience. Don't get so lost in your own visions of what *you* or your group wants to do that you forget what you're trying to communicate or to whom it is being communicated.

Beyond sheer entertainment value, pinpoint an area or topic that would be meaningful to your audience. Choose something that might complement the lesson plans of a curriculum or the overall concerns or struggles your audience might be having or a sermon series by your Vicar. If you're using drama to communicate truth, then you must remain sensitive to *what* truth needs to be communicated.

A couple of cautions, though. Beware of using drama as a weapon for attack or a forum for your personal complaints against your organisation or some of its members. To do so would betray any degree of credibility you might have established besides causing some people to look at you with ill-humour.

T.S. Eliot once said that 'a play should give you something to think about. When I see a play and understand it the first time, then I know it can't be much good.' So you'll want to look for a script that won't be too difficult to understand, yet won't insult your audience's intelligence either; something that explains enough for them to follow along but leaves enough out so they'll have something to think about.

In other words, when you're looking for a script – whether it's comedy or drama – choose one with a prayerful and sensitive heart towards the needs of your audience. The best script will address topics and issues of humanity and Christianity with insight, getting the message across without sacrificing good principles of drama. It's the balance between message and medium that I've mentioned before.

Just as importantly, you'll want a script that is *well-written* in terms of the fundamentals of good drama: story, plot, conflict, character, dialogue, and theme.

What to stay away from
Let's turn this whole thing on its head and consider a few of the negatives – the types of scripts to avoid.

1. Scripts that lack subtlety.
2. Scripts that use characters and dialogue merely as the means to preach a message. Or, to put it another way, scripts that are merely 'adverts for Christ', with all the corresponding depth and dimension. 'Wash those dirty stains out with Christianity! Gets you whiter than white!' Wink, wink. Nudge, nudge.
3. Scripts that preach about specific behaviour. The best dramas explore the *inner* person as seen through action, not the action itself. Whether it's *Hamlet* or *The Full Monty*, we all respond to the *inner* workings of the character's spirit and soul that lead him or her

to take the actions we see. If a person has a drinking problem, we want to know *why* that person drinks so much. What's going on inside the person? The message that excessive drinking is bad for us is not only obvious, but won't work as a dramatic premise for very long. We want to know about the *human condition* that plays out in the course of events. Far too many scripts get lost in personal 'doctrines of lifestyle' rather than Truth and how it applies to the human condition.

4. Scripts that reduce its characters to good guys and bad guys. In real life, we're a little of both. It's tempting in church dramas, for example, to make Christians *right* in what they do and say and those who aren't Christians always *wrong* in what they do and say. Even the Bible gives us balanced portraits of its heroes and saints – why shouldn't our stage productions?

5. Scripts that exploit or sensationalise current topics, trends, or issues.

6. Scripts that try to do *everything*. I once read a sketch that dealt with faith, life after death, a visitation by an angel, prayer, Christian hypocrisy, a philosophical argument about the existence of God, God's intervention in human affairs (why does he let evil persist?), conversion, the horror of war, and healing... all in seven pages. Needless to say, it didn't work.

But these are only a few suggestions about what to watch out for. You'll discern even more as you begin...

Reading scripts for yourself

The only way you're going to make a sound, intelligent decision about the script you use is by doing a lot of script *reading*. The more you read, the better-versed you'll become in the many different forms and styles of playwriting that are out there.

Better still, get out and *see* the plays performed. You'll be inspired and gain insight into what may or may not work for your particular situation.

Bringing them back home

You can read and see all the plays you want but the bigger question is: *can you do them?* Lack of time, talent, and experience could inhibit you and your group from doing the one you'd like to do.

You must constantly ask yourself:

- Does the script fit the goals I've established for my group?
- Is the script appropriate for my audience?
- Do we have the talent to do justice to the characters?
- Do we have the technical resources to stage the script properly?
- Do we have the 'behind-the-scenes' people to stage the play?
- Do we have the proper venue?

As with our discussion of your goals, all of these questions and more must be answered before a play can be selected.

Making changes in the play to suit your needs

You may read a play and believe it would be perfect if you could change a few things. I'm sorry to say that you can't assume you'll be allowed. Any change without permission from the author or publisher is illegal and will infringe on the author's copyright.

Besides that, your changes may unintentionally do serious damage to the play itself. Changing or omitting

lines, portions of plot, or characters may well destroy
the very things that drew you to the play in the first
place.

Are any changes permissible? The only way to know
is to contact the publisher or author of the play, detail
what you would like to change and why, and then wait
for an answer. I would strongly suggest that you make
no plans until you hear for certain whether or not your
changes have been accepted.

Rights and permission

Most plays involve some sort of production/
performance fee (beyond the cost of the individual
copies). Generally such a fee is listed in the front of the
play or can be obtained from the publisher. The fees
vary from play to play.

And don't be tempted to take the 'financial shortcut'
of buying one script and then duplicating it for your
cast and crew. It's not legal and it's certainly not
ethical.

Regrettably, one editor for a mainstream play
publishing house with a religious imprint lamented to
me that of all the schools, amateur and community
theatre groups, and general buyers he deals with,
churches are the worst offenders for illegally
duplicating scripts and not paying production/
performance fees.

There are a lot of excuses for this. Some are even
understandable. 'My church simply can't afford it' or
'It's not *their* work, it belongs to God and we must
share freely' or 'The copyright laws are vague about it
because we're non-profit' or... well, you've heard them.
Maybe you've even used a few of them.

The bottom line is this: if you want quality
Christian material, then somebody has to write it. The
only way anyone can and will write it is if they can

make money off of it to live on. By shirking the appropriate fees or by duplicating books, you are taking away from that person's livelihood. And you know what happens? That person has to quit in order to find a vocation to help pay the bills. And then we're right back at the dilemma found at the beginning of this chapter.

What if I want to do it myself?

Creating your own sketches and plays is certainly a viable alternative. You might surprise yourself. As a personal aside, I began writing scripts for my church out of necessity and never stopped. Many of them are published, enabling me to write professionally. As was true for me, doing it yourself may be your best (and only) option. What should you do?

Though I can't teach you how to write, I *can* give you some cursory suggestions about writing sketches – either by yourself or in the context of your group.

Writing alone

Here's a crash course of things to consider if you're going to try your hand at writing for the stage.

- Should you write a sketch, one-act or full-length play? (Briefly: a sketch sticks to one idea or conclusion, usually in one scene set in one place. A one-act often contains one idea or situation caught in a particular point of time that's played out in more than one scene. A full-length play [two or three acts] traditionally lasts anywhere from ninety minutes to over two hours and can contain multiple ideas, situations and characters played out over any amount of time.)
- *Who* are you writing to? (Who is your audience?)
- *What* are you trying to say? (What's your theme?)

- *How* are you going to say it? (Straight drama? Tragedy? Comedy?)
- *When* and *Where* will it be said? (In church, in a morning service, at an informal talent night?)
- *Why* should anyone care? (Something *every* playwright needs to be concerned about.)
- Whatever you write should have four basic components. A *good premise* with *good characters* and *good dialogue*. And what holds those three elements together is *conflict*.
- Make sure your idea is appropriate for the *stage*. (There are 'closet dramas' that are written for debate and discussion, but not necessarily for the stage.)
- American writing guru Louis Catron teaches that ideas must be 'possible, plausible and probable'.
- Don't procrastinate. Don't second-guess yourself. Just *do it* until you have a first draft. *Then* you can play editor and tear it apart.
- Don't expect to be Shakespeare.
- Take writing courses, read and see plays.

We've already established the need for more Christian playwrights – you could be one of them!

The corporate approach
Creating sketches as a group effort can be a lot of fun if you follow some very basic suggestions.

- Make sure you meet in a setting that is comfortable and away from distractions. If possible, assemble everyone in a circle and give them pads of paper and pens (or designate a fast typist to keep track with a laptop). A running tape recorder may be helpful. Also make room for some improvisation. (Improvisation, if you don't know, is a technique that lets any number of people act out freely an imaginary situation. More about that later.)

- Treat every idea, suggestion, or thought as valid. *Nothing* is allowed to be ridiculed, criticised or corrected – no matter how seemingly stupid or absurd. Sometimes the most ridiculous ideas trigger very good ones.

- Discuss and write down topics and settings regardless of how normal, strange, or mundane they are. Divide paper into two columns. Label one column 'Topic' and the other 'Setting'. List *all* ideas. For instance, the topic might be 'faith' and the setting might be 'a lift'. It might not seem like much until you put two people in a lift talking about the importance of faith – and then the lift breaks down. Other topics could be peer pressure, the meaning of love, jealousy, pettiness, hope, heartbreak, etc. Other settings could be a bus stop or train station, a park bench, a living room, seats at a football match, a church hallway, a school cafeteria, etc. Mix and match the topics and settings. Again, nothing is too outrageous.

- Consider what kinds of characters you want. Who would be appropriate to play out the topics in those particular settings? Have your group members act out (improvise) some of the topics and settings. Let a couple of them (mixing and matching genders, too) play with different types of characters – the school bully, the neurotic web-surfer, the gossipy busybody, the tired housewife, the anxious teenager, the domineering father, etc., and see what you come up with. But don't get lazy. It's easiest to rely on stereotypical characters (like the ones I just listed) while the greater challenge is to come up with unique true-to-life characters.

- Most sketches work best with a 'hook' or a punch-

line at the end. Sometimes it can be an element of
irony, contradiction, or a silly twist. One example of
this is a sketch that has a young man presenting a
list of humorous 'demands' to his Vicar or a 'protest'
will take place in front of the church. After extensive
negotiating, the Vicar tries to diffuse the situation –
but to no avail. Only at the end of the sketch do we
find out that the young man is the Vicar's son.

At some stage past the brainstorming, improvisation
and mucking about, somebody is going to have to put
something on paper so everyone knows what they're
doing. In other words, one lucky person gets to *write*
the sketch. Whether it's handwritten, typed, or word-
processed, your cast needs those magical pieces of
creativity in their hands.

Who gets the honour? Probably the person who was
foolish enough to go to the loo when the vote was
taken.

This is a prime opportunity to enlist the help of that
member of your group who has always enjoyed writing.
You never know how many would-be writers you have
hidden in the woodwork. Now is the time to seek them
out and get them involved.

Polishing the material
Whether it's your own writing or the material created
by your group, you must be a sensitive and sensible
editor. Be objective. Imagine that you are the audience.
Think clearly about what you should keep and what
you should throw out. A bit that seemed outrageously
funny in your head might really be a mere chuckle and
not worth keeping. An idea that had the entire group
in stitches for half an hour may need to be whittled
down to three minutes. Your favourite line in the entire

sketch may have to come out. Be prepared for those possibilities. Nothing you've done is sacred.

And when you've finished the editing, ask yourself: 'Why would anyone *care* to see what we've put together? What's the point?'

Incorporating music into non-musical productions

Like everything else, music is dependent on your talent and resources. You can do a straight play without any music at all or you can do a 'variety show' with songs (original or otherwise) that complement the mood and messages of the sketches. Or you can put together incidental music (guitar, piano or synthesiser) to lead into a sketch or to indicate that a sketch has ended. And then there's always the popular 'musical revue' approach that centres both sketches and songs around a specific theme.

Music is also quite handy as a 'cover' for set changes. Whether you use an instrument, live band or pre-recorded tracks, a song or 'incidental music' can help make set-change time go more quickly for your audience.

Chapter Four: But I'm not a director...

Maybe you think you're not a director. I won't argue with you. But *somebody* has to get the show going and since you're the one reading this book, I'll assume that you got stuck with the job.

Or maybe you *want* to direct. Even though you don't have the education or experience, you have a *heart* for it. That may be as much as you'll need... for now. Know this: it *is* possible for you as a beginner to direct a production, but it won't be easy.

As director, there are a number of things that fall upon your shoulders alone.

- You have to figure out what the sketch or play is about and then guide your group into a clear representation of it on stage.
- You'll have to visualise the setting when no sets are available.
- You'll have to see the characters come to life – how they look, how they speak, *how they think* and why they think that way, how and where they move – *before* a single actor shows up.
- You have to be the eyes of the audience before the audience sees anything.

If the playwright is the composer of a theatrical symphony, then you, as the director, are its conductor.

Directing a production of any sort can be the most frustrating, time-consuming, maddening and *rewarding* experience you'll have.

The director as a reader

As I've suggested already, you would do yourself a great service by reading a variety of plays and studying more detailed texts on directing. You'll do yourself an even greater service by going to as many plays as you can, studying the choices the director made with the characters, line delivery, sets and blocking. How did the director make use of the money? What did the director focus on? How can you adapt some of the ideas? Often such exposure will trigger your own creative juices for your particular production.

Assuming the material you want to perform has been selected, you now need to sit down and read it thoroughly – not as an interested party but *as director*. Read it once for your overall thoughts and reactions. Then read it again for a more critical analysis – pinpointing what the script itself tells you about the story, characters, setting, and theme. Detail your own personal observations and reactions as you consider what the script *doesn't* say directly about those same things. Make notes about potential blocking, light and sound cues, and props. Answer basic questions, like: what *kind* of play is it? Comedy? Drama? Tragedy? Melodrama? Who is the main or primary characters? What do you think and feel about the main character(s)? What is the driving force of the play (what does the main character want? What causes the rising action?)? What is the climax of the play? How does the play appeal to your emotions? How does it appeal to your intellect? How will it ultimately appeal to the eyes of your audience? What do you visualise in your mind as you read it?

Get to know the script as well as you can; you two are going to have to be friends for quite a while.

The director as observer

As director, you need to be an observer in several different ways. I've already mentioned one: going to the theatre. All kinds of theatre. It would also be wise to see some quality films.

Another form of observation is to go to a shopping centre, a bus station, an airport – any place where people abound – and simply *watch* them. (This is an exercise I'll suggest later for your actors.) Watch how they move, talk, and interact. What is unique? What is typical? Apart from being downright interesting, you'll pick up some valuable ideas for your production.

More specific to your role as director will be the necessity of observing your production as a member of the audience would. You, very literally, are the eyes of the audience before the audience ever sees anything. Apart from your own goals for the play, you must anticipate what the audience will be thinking and feeling – and how you can help guide those feelings to a desired end. It's an important duality. You must have the *subjectivity* to work passionately with your material while maintaining the *objectivity* of those who will see it on stage for the first time.

The director as diplomat

Since you'll be dealing with amateur productions, there are a few things beyond the job of directing that you'll need to remember as director.

1. Remember the ongoing battle for credibility. You must be credible not only to the leaders of your organisation, but to your cast and crew. Since you're calling the shots, your cast will have to believe that

you won't let them get up on stage and make fools of themselves. Your crew will have to believe that your decision-making about sets, sound and lights (if you have them) are wise beyond scrutiny. Be sensitive to their scepticism – and don't take it personally.

2. Realise that your cast and crew may not be as dedicated as you are. Chances are, they won't be. That's often how it goes with volunteers. But don't become a martyr with deep guilt-inducing sighs that say 'All right, go ahead and play football instead of coming to rehearsal. I'll rehearse around you... somehow.' Don't be self-righteous with sharp retorts like, 'If *I* can put my time into it, then you can, too!' Remember, unless you're in a paid situation, most of the people are giving up their time to be a part of the production. Every now and again they'll wonder why they're bothering. You'll have to be the one to keep them together – to keep sight of the ultimate purpose of your group. And, more than likely, you'll have to be the one to make up for their lack of commitment. Be patient and don't be too hard on them. Even the disciples slept in the Garden of Gethsemane.

3. Head off the problem of ego and pride at the beginning. The best rule for combating this is the predetermined viewpoint that you and your cast will *do whatever is necessary for the good of the production.* Full stop. World without end. Amen. That means swallowing *your* pride in order to listen open-mindedly to differing viewpoints, massaging bruised egos, offering an apology even when you're not sure it was your fault, and telling them consistently that they're doing a good job even if you don't feel like it any more. But it also means asserting your authority when you have to, making decisions *in spite of* the

ego-politics involved, and often being perceived as the bad guy.
4. Treat the entire cast and crew as if they were the main actors. Obviously, most of your time and attention will go to your leading actors, but it is necessary to balance that with time and attention to everyone as equals. Everyone is important to the success of the production.

The director as picturemaker

What the audience will ultimately see on stage are living pictures. As director, you are the picture-maker. Simplistically put, this means guiding the actors in their movements on (and off) the stage so that, at any point, you could take a picture of them and it would look properly balanced. At its most basic level, you hope your actors can be seen and heard by the audience. Beyond that, you want to create pictures that will enhance your characters, dialogue, scenes and overall goals of production.

The function of moving the characters around is called *blocking*. The script may give you some indication of the blocking; you may also get help from your actors, but a lot of it will be decided by *you* the director.

Why? For one thing, your cast can't see themselves as you can from the audience. They might think where they're standing or how they're moving looks all right – but it could be all wrong for the total picture seen by the audience. Maybe, from the audience's perspective, they can't be seen very well or heard clearly. It's your job to see that they are seen and heard. You're going to turn the play into a series of pictures that will look and sound good. *Blocking* is the way to do it.

If you imagine the stage as a grid of fifteen blocks, here are the traditional areas in which a stage is divided: Up Right, Up Right Centre, Up Centre, Up Left Centre, Up Left, Right, Right Centre, Centre, Left Centre, Left, Down Right, Down Right Centre, Down Centre, Down Left Centre, Down Left. (*Left* and *right* are determined from the actor's viewpoint on the stage looking at the audience.)

Here's your basic vocabulary:

Stage right and *left* (again, from the actor's viewpoint on stage looking at the audience).

Down-stage is 'down' closest to the audience while *up-stage* is further away. Thus, having a character 'moving down-stage' or 'move up-stage' is simply that – moving closer to or away from the audience. (To appease the two purists who are still reading this text, the 'up' and 'down' refer to stages which, during Shakespeare's day, were sloped from high in the back to low toward the audience. This was a very utilitarian way of improving sight-lines for the audience.)

Off-stage takes your character away from the centre of the stage while *on-stage* moves them closer to the centre.

Since most of us are more attuned to television or films rather than theatre, we're used to the camera directing our eyes. It's easy, then, to forget that there must be a centre of attention on the stage or *emphasis*. Without proper emphasis, the audience could become easily confused about where they should be looking. You as the director must help them to see what character or area of the stage should command their attention at any specific moment.

One way to achieve proper sight and sound for your audience is in the proper placement of your actor's body positions on stage. Your actor could stand *full-front*, facing the audience. Or taking a *one-quarter* turn to the left or right. Or stand *profile* to the audience. Or take a *three-quarter* turn away to the left or right away from the audience. Or take the *full-back* position, with his or her back facing the audience.

I have it from several good sources that the positions from strongest to weakest for your audience are: full-front, one-quarter, profile, three-quarter and, obviously, full-back. In fact, the full-back is more than just weak, it's almost a sin. Except in the most remarkable circumstances with the most gifted actors, full-back not only makes it impossible for your audience to see the actor's face, but obliterates their chance of hearing any lines spoken.

Another thing to consider is that standing or sitting is generally stronger than kneeling or lying down. Also, the position of the head will greatly affect the strength or weakness of body positions.

With two actors on stage, your picture becomes more complicated and their positions become increasingly important. There are a few traditional terms for their positions. Imagine a straight line running from stage left to stage right. If you have two actors standing parallel on that line in a one-quarter turn, it's called *sharing*. If the two actors face one another, it's called *profile*. When one actor is up-stage facing the audience and another actor is down-stage facing away from the audience, you have the potential for *up-staging*. Up-staging occurs when our attention goes to the wrong actor because of his or her positioning. For example, if John is the character with whom we are concerned, and what he is saying is most important to the scene, then he should be up-stage facing the audience and Nigel, the second character, should be in the 'weak' position down-stage with his back to us. To have it the other way around would diminish our ability to see and hear John. Up-staging is also a popular term for those times when an actor takes the attention away from the actor who *should be* seen and heard (often through distracting actions or mannerisms).

And what if you have more than two people on stage at the same time? Then you must position them in such a way that the audience won't be looking over the entire stage trying to figure out who they should be watching.

This can be accomplished in several different ways. One way is through *lines* created by the bodies of the actors across the stage – straight, curved, diagonal or broken up. A second way is the popular *triangle* where two of the characters are towards the audience with a third further away from the audience in the centre. A third way is to place the actors around the stage so that *their* focus of attention must be on the primary character (two to one side facing the speaker centre or down right, etc). A fourth way is to use your common sense. Look at the scene and notice where *your* eyes go naturally.

And that's a good summation for the entire process of blocking: make sure that it is *practical*. Can your actors be seen? Can they be heard? Do they look natural and comfortable? Are their positions complementary to their characters and the scene?

That is the essence of making pictures for your audience.

The director as mover

Apart from still-life pictures, blocking involves *movement*: the actions your actors take while on-stage. Some of the stage movements will be obvious from the script. It'll tell you where the character should go and it should be fairly clear *why* they went there (no actor should ever enter, exit or move around the stage without a specific reason).

Other stage movements will be *implied* in the script. It might not say so directly but you *know* that the only way Auntie Millicent is going to give Little Johnny that drink is to have her walk over and give it to him.

There are some stage movements that won't be stated or implied but will be born out of necessity for practical or technical reasons – to get the actors where they need to be for a line or scene, to allow them to be seen and heard, to keep them out of the way of entering or exiting characters, to heighten comedy, to heighten the drama and emotion, to supplement dialogue, to keep your picture in order. These situations will require creativity on your part, to understand and interpret the play well enough to sort out the non-specified movements, to complement and enhance the story, to convey its mood, to communicate the truth of its characters.

You must ask yourself: where is the scene taking place and what would be the normal activity there? What is the emotional focus of the scene and how would the characters move in it (a funeral would have to be handled differently from an office party, for example)? If it is a scene with a lot of dialogue, would movement help break up the potential monotony of 'talking heads'?

But before you have your characters bouncing off of the ceiling in frenzied activity, there are a few things you should know about stage movement:

1. A moving character will attract attention away from the character standing still. Therefore, actors should only move on their own lines and with a specific purpose behind the movement (to give emphasis to the character or line, to draw the audience *away* from another part of the stage for some reason, or to draw the audience's attention *to* another part of the stage.
2. If the character speaking is to cross in front of another character, it should always be down-stage from him or her.

3. Don't let your actors make the very normal mistake of moving in a way that puts their backs to the audience or their faces away from the audience. It's easy to forget good body positions when moving – watch them closely.

4. Movement can be critical to establishing or amplifying emotion, showing changes in characters or relationships, altering the direction of mood, dialogue or thought in a scene, revealing character, or setting up a line. You must ask yourself *who* should be moving, *what* kind of moving should they do, *when* should they move, *where* should they move to, *why* are they moving at all, and *how* should they move?

5. Movement should break up potential monotony. And it should have enough variety to keep from becoming monotonous itself.

The director as improviser

If you find that your stage consists of nothing more than the space between the lectern and the pews, then take these same principles and apply them there. Whatever stage you must use, the actors must be seen and heard or there's no point in doing the sketch at all. As director you should sit in various places around the nave to make sure that pillars won't obscure the line of sight, or that the natural acoustics won't turn voices into nothing but distant echoes, or that your brilliant blocking and staging ideas won't disappear because someone in the first row has big hair.

A final word

This chapter is not (and could not be) the complete word on directing. It's a starting point. I suggest you browse through your local bookshop to find more detailed works about the theory and practical sides of directing.

Chapter Five: Choosing your cast

You've made your decision about what you're going to perform. Whether you're leading a drama group that meets on a regular basis, or are assembling a group for a specific task, you need to decide on the actors who will bring the script to life.

There are two ways to do this:

1. You may choose the people based on your personal knowledge of their abilities and their rightness for a role.
2. You can conduct *auditions*.

The personal approach

Sometimes you may not want to open the production or group to everyone. You know that George over there would be perfect for the part and don't need to consider anyone else. Or Janet has always shown an instinctive ability for acting and should be a part of your group. It happens that way sometimes and, in the face of such clear choices, auditions may be unnecessary. You can then talk individually with your potential actors, in a 'private audition', getting their feelings about the role or group and how they might be involved.

There are advantages and disadvantages to this type

of casting. A disadvantage is that, without meaning to, you may limit yourself, your characters, and your group by going with people you know. It is too often the easy way out of stretching beyond your immediate circle of friends and acquaintances. You take the chance of losing your open-mindedness to outsiders and objectivity about the direction of your group or production. And there will be those who'll complain that you're not being open-minded or fair.

The advantage to this approach is that you get exactly who you want without the fuss of auditions. Hand-picked, you'll get people who are more in line with your goals, the vision you have for the group or production, and your personality (never underestimate the damage that can be wreaked by simple personality conflicts).

Getting ready for auditions

Allowing that you've decided to do auditions, there are several ways to go about it. One way is to meet the candidate privately, ask her to perform something to show off her skills, talk to her about your goals for the production, and then ask her to read for a specific character from the script. Another way to audition is to conduct what is traditionally called a 'cattle call'. That's where you put out the word that you want to audition actors and they come *en masse*.

Either way you choose, here are some tips about preparing yourself.

First, you need to know what you're looking for in terms of your characters (see the chapter about acting to help you with this). Make a list with any specific notes you've made on the characters. Select key portions of the script for your participants to act out. What sections will reveal the most about the character and the person auditioning for it? Consider the different moods and demands the script makes on the actor. Also, it's not uncommon to ask the participants to come prepared with something of their own to show off their skills.

Put together a form for your participants to fill out. Include a space for names, addresses, contact phone numbers, e-mail addresses, age, height, weight, hair colour, specific talents, availability, and a space at the bottom for any notes you want to make during the audition.

Decide in what order you want to audition the various characters. I suggest you do it one character at a time, beginning with your principal characters and working down the list to the secondary characters. In the case of a general audition, you may want to mix and match the various actors to see how they interact with each other as various characters. Consider their physical appearances – height, family resemblance, etc.

Make copies of the relevant pages for the relevant characters, or use a couple of copies in the audition itself. Your decision will depend on whether or not you want the actors to read them in advance, while they're waiting, or if you want a cold, first-time reading.

Finally, you must decide on a venue for the auditions. Somewhere comfortable for both you and the would-be actors that's not too crowded (in the case of a general audition) is preferable. And, of course, you want plenty of space for the actors to *act*.

When you think you're ready, announce the audition's date, time and place through newsletters, fliers, posters, verbal announcements, etc. Then brace yourself.

Auditions: doing them

At the beginning of an audition, make sure you do all you can to help the participants relax. Begin with a few warm-up exercises or improvisations. Maintain an upbeat and positive attitude.

There are two ways to conduct the main auditions. One is to audition everyone together in a large room or auditorium. (Some of your would-be actors may find this intimidating.) The alternative would be to call the actors into a smaller room individually or in pairs. You'll have to decide which works best based on your casting needs.

Generally, though, you'll call the name of the participant, and ask him or her to read the pre-selected scene or scenes either alone or with other participants. You'll want to explain the scene to them briefly, take notes about their basic acting ability – how they did and whether you need them for 'call-backs' (meaning that you want to see them again because they were good), and finish with a very polite and encouraging 'Thank you'.

In the midst of all this, you must remain objective throughout the process and never betray to anyone that you've made some sort of mental decision until *everyone* has auditioned. You must also make it clear that there are a lot of factors involved and that no one will automatically get a role if they read well or not get a role if they don't. A lot of fragile egos are on the line here so always be tactful, reassuring, and diplomatic.

It's also important to make sure everyone understands the kind of schedule you're planning and some of the expectations you have for the production. This might eliminate a few people immediately if they have conflicting commitments.

Here are some of the questions you must consider while auditioning...

• Is there something about the actor's personality that seems to match the character's?

- What about the actor's appearance, voice, and speech? Did the actor speak clearly with good projection?
- What kind of stage presence and poise does the actor have? Does the actor show strength or weakness, confidence or insecurity?
- Was the actor's reading 'functional' or did the actor intuitively grasp the character and dialogue?

Be aware with readings, though, that you can have someone who reads horribly the first time but excels once he's 'warmed-up' to it and others who read extremely well but never grow beyond the initial effort.

Once you narrow the choices down, bring the actors back for a final reading to see how the entire group looks before making any announcements. At this point, you may present a more detailed explanation of your expectations and their obligations in schedule and time.

You should also consider whether or not you want to have *understudies* (these are the people who play 'stand-by' to your main actors in case something happens to keep them away from rehearsals or the actual performance). If you have understudies for all of the main characters, you can often have them prepare for a second role. The problem is finding someone who is willing to put in the time and energy for what may be a fruitless role.

Behind the scenes decision-making
For the sake of your production or group, there are things you have to ask yourself privately about the people who have auditioned – questions that go beyond what you saw on stage.

- Will the people *really* commit themselves to the production's rehearsal schedule and performances? What is their pattern of commitment to other activities? Do they begin a project enthusiastically only to drop out in the middle?
- If they *are* committed, is it also possible that they're *over*committed (are they involved in so many things that they couldn't possibly do the best job in your production or group)? Will they be conscientious?
- Will they co-operate and follow your direction?
- By virtue of their personality, will they add or distract from rehearsals?
- What is their temperament?
- Are their expectations of the production or group realistic? (They may expect even more than you do and get frustrated when you don't live up to those expectations.)
- Will you have a power struggle with them?
- How are their memorisation skills?
- What are their reasons for joining your group? Do you think they're joining just to 'get in the spotlight'?
- What are the personal ramifications of choosing this person over another person?
- How are they perceived by other members in your group? By other leaders?
- If you've auditioned children, are you also prepared to deal with their parents for the length of the production? (You *must* consider this. You won't have one without the other.)

Once you've made your decisions, know clearly in your mind why you've made them and be prepared to articulate those thoughts to your candidates.

Communicating the decisions

One way to communicate your decisions is to post them in a prearranged and conspicuous place – a notice board, newsletter, flier, etc.

Another way to communicate your decisions is to send out letters with the announcements of who has been assigned the parts, and include thanks to everyone who auditioned.

Still another way is to make personal phone calls or face-to-face appointments. The drawback to this one, however, is that you put yourself in the very uncomfortable position of answering '*why* Judith got the part and I didn't'.

I would suggest that you avoid announcing role assignments in youth group meetings. The one who didn't receive a part may feel devastated when they find out. This feeling is intensified when others are around to hear the decisions. It can be embarrassing for all concerned.

It's your choice. Whatever you do, be kind and encouraging. Assure the participants that the decision was made for a variety of reasons and was not necessarily because of a lack of talent or ability.

Living with your decisions

Once you've made your selections for the group or the production, I suggest that you leave town, or if that isn't possible, disconnect the phone and hide in the shed for a few weeks. Johnny might be a little hurt that he didn't get the part but Johnny's *parents* might be inclined to stalk you. Words and phrases like 'narrow-minded', 'tyrant', 'my cat could direct better than you', 'pre-casting' and 'it'll be a horrible show' will be sent your way. Count on it.

Be gentle, civilised, and intelligent in your responses

and you may make it through with minimal physical
damage.

What about the rest of them?

Apart from yourself and your actors, who will help you?

You can't do all of the work. Hopefully, you won't
have to. I heartily recommend that you get someone
with organisational skills to assist you. This person can
create a list of members' names, addresses, and phone
numbers, etc. – or help to call all members for
meeting/rehearsal arrangements – or handle any of the
other details that'll steal your time from creatively
directing your production. If you can't find such a
person, then be prepared for a few late nights doing
them yourself. Know that such organisation is
necessary for the effective functioning of your group or
production. Otherwise, you'll be banging your head
against the proverbial wall and your cast and crew will
slowly desert you. Nobody likes to think they're
wasting their time.

Finding people to handle building sets, co-
ordinating sound or lights – all the technical people
who work behind the scenes – probably won't be easy.
More than likely you'll be involved in all aspects. For
sets and other stage details, your cast will have to help.
But sound and lights? Those may be the most difficult
of all.

If your school or church is fairly advanced in areas
of light and sound, then go to that department and
find out how to get these people involved.

If not, then you may have to make a plea to your
sponsoring organisation through the usual methods.
Maybe there are a couple of people with interests in
those areas. Or it's possible that one or two of the
people who auditioned and *didn't* get parts will be able
to help. Otherwise, you may have to ask specific people

directly to help – whether they know anything about it or not.

Whoever you try to involve, you must ask yourself many of the same questions about them as you did for the actors.

- Does he have a special talent that matches the job?
- Can she get along with others?
- Does he take suggestions willingly?

Battling the bureaucracy

Depending on the size of your organisation, you'll have to juggle your production or group against any number of other activities. Check the master-schedule thoroughly. Take absolutely *nothing* for granted or you'll show up for rehearsal only to discover that you are without a meeting place, or half of your cast and crew, because of a conflicting event.

Be sure your meeting place is suitable for an *acting* group. The room should be large and spacious enough for actors to move about freely during acting and improvisation exercises. If the room is too small or if you find yourself dodging tables every time you meet, you'll have trouble.

Be diplomatic with the person in charge of co-ordinating meeting times and places. If you have a lot of difficulties with the schedule or facilities, they will certainly show up in the morale of your group and the quality of your production. Play by the rules but go to the highest authority if the rules keep working against you.

The hard part

For some, the auditions and initial organising are the hard parts. I'm worn out just writing about it all. But take heart. The really fun and creative part can now start...

Chapter Six: Acting and training actors

Acting is a peculiar activity with equally peculiar contradictions. And the people in amateur theatres represent them all. You'll find those who 'live for acting' but couldn't act to save their lives. You'll find others who wouldn't imagine trying to act – in fact, they might be the *least* likely to do it – yet there's something that *clicks* for them on stage and they're wonderful. There are those who will *insist* that they can't act and guess what? They're absolutely right. They can't. The list goes on and on. You'll get to meet all of these people eventually.

You'll have to.

Because, when all the planning, directing, rehearsing, sweating, time and effort are done, it's what happens on stage that matters. Your production will rise or fall based on the actors you have there. It's up to the actor to take on the burden of bringing the character to believability – to *life* – while accurately representing the author's intent and the director's interpretation. The actor gets both the joy and frustration of being creative and imaginative but *within the confines* of the play's requirements.

Actors have to try to get the audience to respond even if the audience doesn't want to. They have to *win* them. Sometimes they'll make it and sometimes they won't. But, if you're the director, you and your actors will know you've all done your best. This chapter will give you some help in bringing out the best in your actors.

Speech, speech!

Unless you're a mime artist, all the great acting in the world won't mean much unless you can be heard and understood. Poor pronunciation (depending on characterisation), mumbling, slurring, talking too fast, talking too slow, talking too soft (or the fear of talking *too* loud), unintentional heavy accents, and other similar problems can destroy a production. This seems to be especially true for youth groups since many of its members lack experience in acting or speaking in front of people. They shuffle about and mumble in a low near-whisper for fear that they're talking *too* loudly...

One of the biggest problems is that most beginners don't learn how to use the *diaphragm* correctly, with deep and controlled breathing to get all of the way to the end of the sentence (go ahead, try *that* sentence and see how you do). Such control is the essence of *projection* and will make all the difference in keeping actors heard in the balconies and preventing them from becoming hoarse. The power behind the voice must originate in the breathing, not in the throat, and involves inhaling more actively than in normal speech and exhaling with more controlled pressure. Sound confusing? There are a lot of good books available for a more detailed explanation and exercises, or ask a local voice instructor.

Another problem with most beginners is a lack of *articulation* – using the mouth, tongue and teeth to say the words properly and clearly. That involves relaxing the jaw, opening the mouth wide, and moving the tongue and lips to produce very distinct sounds. It's a

safe bet that most beginners are afraid to do this
because it feels funny. Most of us don't make our
mouths go that wide or speak so clearly in normal
conversation. But dialogue is *not* normal conversation
and, to be heard, good articulation *must* be achieved.
It's worth remembering that, though it may *feel* funny,
it won't *look* funny to the audience. In fact, it'll look
quite natural.

Here are a few exercises to help with speech.

- Achieve physical relaxation through tightening the
  body muscles. Have your actors lie down and
  tighten the muscles until they're as tense as possible,
  then relax them suddenly. Work from the tips of the
  toes to the top of the head, alternately tightening
  and relaxing muscles.
- Bounce around with their arms and head moving
  freely and loosely.
- Have them slowly roll their heads around their
  shoulders in a complete circle, first clockwise, then
  anti-clockwise.
- Yawn. As long, deeply and loudly as possible.
- Exhale deeply and loudly through the vocal cords.
- Repeat the phrase 'The teeth, the lips, the tip of the
  tongue', increasing in speed and precision each
  time.

There are many others, but these will be helpful for
starters.

Once more with feeling

If the director is responsible for guiding the production
into a powerful representation of the play or sketch,
then it is the actor's responsibility ultimately to *make it
work* emotionally for the audience.

The interpretation of the character's lines by the

director and actor will help clarify the line's meaning, enhance the character, express the line's emotional intent while leading to the climax and, hopefully, lend variety to the play.

Making sure the audience understands the meaning and feeling of the lines can be achieved by some very obvious means.

1. There are four elements to using one's voice: pitch, volume, tempo, and quality. *Pitch* is the highness or lowness of sound, *volume* is loudness, *tempo* is the rate, and *quality* is the timbre that distinguishes one voice from another. Each one of these four elements can be used to one's advantage for interpreting lines. Changing any one of these elements can heighten or diminish emotion. For example, a higher pitch can show high emotion and excitement while a lower pitch can create the sound of authority, deep emotion, depression or anything God-like (that's a joke). The same is true for increases or decreases in volume or tempo. Practise talking fast and loud in front of the mirror and see if someone doesn't ring the police.

2. Emphasis. Sometimes a word. Sometimes an entire line. Say the sentence 'What's that on the road ahead?' Now say it this way: 'What's that on the road *ahead*?' What's the difference? The difference is in which word or words are emphasised in the line. Emphasis gives meaning to words in the context of lines, and the lines in the context of scenes, and the scenes in the context of the total play. What's the right emphasis? Most scripts will indicate emphasis by underlining or italicising key words. Other times, it'll be implied. If not, then it'll be up to you to understand your character and the scene well enough to *know* what's appropriate. How does it

sound if different words are emphasised? Which one sounds correct? You can draw attention to a particular word or line or take away from its importance by how you emphasise it (or don't) through a rise or fall in pitch, change in volume or tempo, or pausing right before the word or line is delivered.

3. Inflection – a change in pitch in the word being said. It can rise at the end, fall at the end, or do both within the word. This can be a big problem for beginners since we're inclined to *act* the same way we *read*. For some reason we end each sentence or question with the same inflection, with little or no variety. This can be boring and monotonous. Consider the thought, emotion, and speech patterns of the character within the scene.

4. Pause. This one can be difficult since many beginners are more interested in getting their lines said and getting *off* the stage rather than taking the time for good, effective pauses. Absolute fear of silence on the actor's part might destroy one of the most effective tools you have. The pause, when handled properly, can be just as powerful as any line delivered. A pause speaks volumes as long as it is justified and in keeping with the character.

5. Rhythm. This is determined by the spacing between words and the frequency in delivery, how pauses are used, the emotional direction of the line and, as much as anything, whatever sounds natural and appropriate.

6. Responding. To put it simply, actors must be good listeners. These things apply not only to the actor's lines but to how the actor responds to other characters' lines. Acting is more than simply waiting for someone else to finish her lines so you can say yours. The actor must be attentive and perceptive to

what she's saying and how she's saying it so she can discern how to deliver her line in character.

Beware of the 'typical' approach to how lines are delivered. We all fall into the trap of taking the standard route rather than the correct one. A line that calls for anger is too often delivered by shouting. That's easy. And it's a sure sign of inexperience. A lack of acting experience combined with the demand for strong emotion on stage sometimes produces *extreme* emotion. For example, a character required to cry is often portrayed by heavy sobbing and wailing. A laugh that should have been a chuckle becomes an outburst. Beware of the obvious.

What a character!

Effective characterisation on stage can open the door for a myriad of interpretations, discussions, debates, and even estrangement between actor and director, actor and other actors, and actor and the playwright's solicitor. Regardless, the actor's mission is to figure out *who* the character is and how to properly represent him or her on stage. There are several sources for determining this: the script, the director, outside resources and the actor's own imagination.

From the script, answer these questions:

- Why is the character in the play at all? How does the character fit in with the overall premise and action of the play?
- Is the character realistic or a caricature?
- What does the character want? What motivates or drives the character throughout the play?
- What does the character do in the play? What kinds of action does the character take?
- What does the character say about himself? What do

the other characters say about the character? How
does the character relate to other characters? Who
are the character's friends? Who are the character's
enemies?

- What does the character look like? How old is the
  character? How does the character speak? Walk?
  Stand? Any noticeable physical traits?
- What is the character's family background? Religious
  background? Education? Economic background?
  Emotional background? Politics?
- What made the character who he is by the time we
  see him in the play?
- What are the character's attitudes towards different
  topics? What does the character like or dislike?
- Why do you think the character is who he is? What
  kind of adjectives would you use to describe the
  character?
- What will the character become by the end of the
  play? Is the character different at the end from how
  he was at the beginning? Why?
- Write an imaginary biography with as much detail
  as possible.

You, the director, are another source of determining
character qualities. The actor must be open to your
interpretation and thoughts – whether he agrees or
disagrees with them. Unless the actor can argue
something specific from the script itself, the actor must
yield for the sake of harmony in your production. You
as the director must have the final word. However,
listen attentively and *discuss* various interpretations to
see which one will work best for the production. On
the other hand don't let the actor count on you for
every detail and nuance. Those are things only the
actor can give. As an effective director, though, you will

have to give time and a creative rehearsal environment in which to experiment.

Outside resources can be very informative about character. A little research will go a long way if you can find articles, reviews, and critiques of the play you're doing. Or if you're doing a play based on some point in history, then research that period, find out what was happening and why, and then try to understand how that character fits into it. Sometimes there's a lot more there than even the playwright may have realised.

When all is said and done, there's only the actor. The actor is going to have to make the character real – first for himself, then for you the director, and then the audience. Because if the actor doesn't believe it, he's going to have a hard time convincing anyone else.

An actor should ask: How much is the character like me? How am I different? Do I *like* the character? Why or why not? These are questions to help the actor find the character within himself.

An important key for discovering how to play the character is through *observing*. In life, through friends and acquaintances, strangers, everyday happenings, sitting in a public place and watching people as they pass, through literature, films, television... these things can combine to give insight and inspiration for the character.

Acting

Earlier I called acting an activity of contradictions. Acting *methods* fit nicely into that category as well. If you want to learn about acting, there are a lot of so-called experts who will go to their theatrical deaths claiming they have the better way for you to do it. Sadly, though, I've seen an entire cast become completely neurotic about their production because they had just enough 'method acting' to make them dangerous. They twisted, poked, probed, and scrutinised their characters until they couldn't make them out at all.

Ultimately your actor is going to have to work out the best way to bring a character to life for your audience. Good acting is good acting no matter how you get there. Think, imagine, and experiment to get to the heart of the character, and once that's done, stick with it. In rehearsals, have your actors concentrate on staying 'in character' – even if there are distractions or other actors fall out of character. As you get closer to the actual performance date, be sure your actors polish and refine their characters. They'll grow as the actor grows.

One practical way to do that is by insisting that your actors are *prepared* for rehearsals. They (and you) won't get the full benefit of rehearsals if they're trying to concentrate on that scene they should have already memorised while you're trying to get them to concentrate on blocking for the next scene.

Encourage your actors to *be natural*. If they're uncomfortable, your audience will be uncomfortable, too. If their performances are unrealistically rendered or exaggerated (except for certain comic situations), your audience will dismiss the characters as unbelievable or inaccessible. Whether they intend to or not, the actors may tell the audience that they don't really belong up there on stage, they're just playing parts. The goal is to make the audience believe that they *are* the characters. So, being *natural* is an extension of being thoroughly in character, comfortable with the lines, and completely focused on the surroundings and how they fit into them. It's easy for some people – they seem to have an intuitive ability for getting on stage and making it look easy. For most, though, it takes hard work and experience.

I've heard it said that all acting is about *sincerity*: if you can fake that, you've got it made.

Memorising lines

Your actors should start memorising their lines as soon as possible. Here are several helpful suggestions you can give them:

- Highlight your lines with a highlighting pen or marker. This will help you visualise your script in your mind.
- Go through the script page by page until you know the lines.
- Place a sheet of paper on the page and work your way down, keeping your lines covered, until you know them.
- Go over your lines with other people in the play or a friend who will read with you.

Hands off!

One obvious difference between a good actor and a novice is that a good actor knows what to do with his hands. The novice simply can't figure out what to do with those blasted things at the end of his arms: put them in his pockets? Fold them across his chest? Clasp them behind his back? Put them on his hips?

The answer – as is true with *anything* to do with acting – depends on the character. If the character is nervous, then the hands, and the actor's entire body, will reflect that nervousness. If the character is confident, then the hands will move decisively and appropriately, even when nothing seems to be happening.

Rehearse what your actors do with their hands. Don't leave it to chance. Work closely with all of your beginning actors on the use of their hands – and their bodies.

Callisthenics

There are some rather strange things your actors can do to 'exercise' for acting. They're strange because your actors may feel awfully silly if someone walks in on them... but they're effective to stretch the *acting muscles* a little bit. Tell your actors to:

1. Practise a variety of facial expressions in front of a mirror. Often the face you *think* you're making isn't the one you're really making. Look closely at what your face does when you're trying to frown, or cry, or laugh, or chuckle... try a whole spectrum of emotions. Videotape this, if you can.
2. Practise laughing by thinking of the funniest things you can – an incident, a joke you once heard, a bit from a TV show or movie. Practise making your laugh sound spontaneous and natural.
3. Practise crying by recalling something that makes you sad – real or imaginary. Concentrate on a distinct pain you've experienced. Recall how it felt and what it did to you emotionally and physically.
4. Imagine yourself in a particular location – your favourite place from childhood, for example. Close your eyes and imagine it all around you. Use your senses to recreate it in your mind. Imagine you are touching the things that surround you, imagine the sounds that filled the place, imagine the smell, the taste of it.
5. Imagine holding something in your hands that you treasured (and possibly lost) at least five years ago. See it in your mind – what it looked like – and concentrate on what it feels like to hold it again. What emotions do you feel?

6. Go to a bus station, shopping centre, busy street – anywhere where there's a lot of people – and simply observe. Watch the people walk, inter-relate, conduct themselves. Notice their facial expressions, voices, and attitudes. Do you see anything interesting? Is there anyone or anything you can mimic or imitate?

7. Choose an object in nature (tree, flower, etc) and try to physically recreate its growth from when it was a seed.

8. Recreate a scene in your mind of something that has happened that day (going to the refrigerator, getting the milk container out, pouring the milk into a glass, etc). Then act that scene out in slow motion. Are you able to keep a consistent speed? Does it look and feel real?

9. Observe, then mimic, the actions of some of your favourite animals.

Improvisation

Unlike acting exercises, improvisation is more focused in its structure. You or your actors will take an imaginary situation or conflict and improvise (hence the name) all of the lines and action. It isn't easy but it's worthwhile for developing skills in character and believability.

Some basic rules for improvisation:

• The best improvisation completely pantomimes holding objects or props.
• React *and* initiate action – don't do all of one or the other.
• Minimal or no physical contact.
• Always have a starting point. Don't worry about a specific ending. Give a set amount of time at the beginning or simply end it when it begins to drag.

- Keep the energy high at all times.

Now, here are a few ideas for you to improvise. Remember to keep the group's energy up. If things begin to slow down, quickly insert someone else into the scene or stop it and start another. The director's role is critical. Let's give it a try:

1. Two people meet in a bargain basement. An imaginary table piled high with scarves sits in the centre. A casual conversation ensues until both find a scarf they like. When they pull it out, they discover they are holding opposite ends of the same scarf. A 'heated' discussion begins.
2. Two people are watching television in the lounge area of a college dormitory. A third person enters and interrupts their viewing by trying to sell them something.
3. One person is the head of a 'customer service' department in a large department store. Any number of people come by, one at a time, trying to return merchandise.
4. A young man with a sizeable opinion of himself takes a young lady out – one he wants to impress. The date is at a restaurant that he thinks is the best but, to the girl, it's a real dive, complete with obnoxious waitress.
5. A young couple are on their honeymoon at a beach. A conversation ensues and, as they talk, they are asked to switch emotions on cue while maintaining a reasonable amount of sense in the conversation. Emotions to use: giddy joy, distrust, worry, laughter, sarcasm, despair, stubbornness, forgiveness.
6. Take a section from a famous play or movie and have an individual read it normally. Then alter

how it is read by having him or her do it in different styles: Shakespearean, as an Australian soap opera, as a Western, as a news reporter, etc.

7. A young man takes his fiancée out to dinner the night before the wedding, only to tell her he's not going through with it. (Then reverse these roles.)

8. Noah is building the ark and his disgruntled wife comes out and asks him what he's doing, complains that none of the other work is getting done around the house, etc.

9. A husband and wife with two young children are on their way to a counsellor to learn about family unity. What happens in the car exposes their need for the counsellor.

10. Two people are sitting on a park bench, each waiting to meet their 'date' for the evening. In the process of their conversation, they discover – to their horror – that they're both waiting for the *same* person.

11. A couple are on their first date to a cinema. In his haste to make a good impression, he does everything wrong – from spilling popcorn in her lap to hitting her in the face while trying to put his arm around her (be careful).

12. A person visits a psychiatrist because every time he coughs he starts to laugh uncontrollably – until he sneezes, when he instantly stops laughing. (This can be expanded by having the person cry whenever the word 'you' is said and then stop on a finger snap.)

13. A girl (or boy) was supposed to go out with a friend but ditches him or her because she'd received a more interesting offer to go to a party. Suddenly the two meet *at the party*.

14. A shy young girl of sixteen is caught shoplifting. While being questioned, we discover she is

actually from a wealthy family and why she stole the merchandise.

15. Three people are trapped in a lift. Realising they are stuck there for an indefinite time, their conversation covers everything from a hopeful rescue to 'black humour' to resolute despair.

Acting exercises

Along with the improvisation suggestions, here are a few acting exercises to try with your group:

1. Have your actors impersonate (accurately, not cruelly) someone they know from their past. Have the group ask this person questions about who they are, what they do, how they know the person impersonating them, etc.
2. Cut out magazine pictures of interesting-looking people – without names – and hand them out. Each member must then stand up and use their imaginations to portray the person in the picture.
3. Come up with a variety of situations, conflicts, confrontations, embarrassments, familiar play or movie scenes, personal experiences, and have different members act them out.
4. Put everyone in a circle (or two or three if your group is large) and have them talk one at a time to the person on their right as if that person were someone else, someone not necessarily known by the group but from the individual's past or present that conjures up positive or negative emotions (a long-lost friend, someone who hurt them at some point, etc). The person being spoken to must do their best – without knowing who they are – to react, ask questions, and try to figure out what's going on.
5. Have everyone write down one sentence on a card,

it could be anything ('How are you today?' or 'The cow jumped over the moon' etc), then mix the sentences up. Hand two or three of them out to a couple of your members. Have your actors create a scene from it.

6. A commonly-used exercise is called 'Fall Into The Circle'. This is where a group of six or eight people forms a tight circle. A volunteer steps to the centre of the circle, closes his eyes and allows himself to fall stiff-legged backwards. The people in the circle gently push him back and forth to one another, *never* allowing him to fall. You must be very careful with this, making sure that no one in the group would think it funny to let the person hit the ground. When done properly, this exercise can teach a lot about trust and relaxation.

7. Blindfold one person. Have another person lead the 'blind' one around the room or over an obstacle course. At various points, the blind person should be given objects to touch and describe. This can be a great deal of fun *and* heighten sensory perception.

8. Line your group up into four or more parallel lines with everyone an arm's length apart with arms raised to shoulder level. Two volunteers begin slowly walking between the two rows. The director loudly says 'Streets' and the people in the lines do a quarter turn to their right, or 'Avenues' in which they go back a quarter turn to the left – arms still extended. The two walking through must change direction as the lines change. Apart from trying to get through the maze, this teaches both the couple and the people in the lines how to create a quick, common and co-ordinated response.

9. Divide your group into couples and have one person in each couple become a mirror. Every move

the one person makes, the other person must copy. The individuals should be encouraged to do this at varied speeds and with varied size of movement.

10. Have everyone get into a crouched position. On the count of three, they should 'explode' into a position they hold. Slowly, almost imperceptibly, begin to change position into something else. This is an incredible and challenging exercise for body control and concentration.

These are only a few acting exercises. More can be found in books on acting technique at your local bookshop, or a shop that specialises in theatre publications.

Chapter Seven: Production! Props, make-up, sound, lighting, set, publicity ...

You have your script in hand. You have your actors in place. Now we need to turn our attention to the other aspects of your production. Before I get to details, it's worth remembering three basic rules for your production.

1. Keep it simple. Simplicity in production is often one of the first keys to success in amateur (and many professional) productions. Often, more can be accomplished with two folding chairs and two actors than a detailed set with backdrop, smoke machines, live animals, and a cast of thousands. (Not that you'll have the budget or access to any of those things anyway.)
2. Keep it clean. It's the little things like tidiness on stage that separates second-rate amateur productions from those that are first-rate. This is particularly true in a fast-paced, short-sketch format, where chairs and props are moved and removed rapidly. You don't want people tripping over the clutter.
3. Keep it moving. This is not referring to pacing of the actors or their line delivery but to those moments between scenes or sketches where bodies, props and set pieces are being moved. This must be done quickly, quietly, and efficiently. It is surprising how

a production can be well-conceived, well-written and well-acted, but come to a grinding halt because the production pacing isn't what it should be. This principle is best accomplished by either having a small 'stage' crew expressly assigned to clean and reset the stage, or, in the case of small productions, the cast should be given the production tasks such as removing chairs, adjusting microphones or handling props. These assignments should be rehearsed as diligently as any acting scene. And it's worth mentioning again the value of simple underscoring for scene changes.

The whole premise of a quality production is to enhance the focus of the script. That being the case, let's talk about some key elements of a good production.

Props, a treatise on canes, and costumes

Props (short for *properties*) are items which, hopefully, bring realism to the stage and help transport the audience to the time or location where the action occurs. These include *set props* (large items like furniture, rugs, curtains, trees, rocks, etc), *trim props* (small items added to decorate, etc), and *hand props* (smaller items often carried or used by the actors themselves).

Props are there to enhance and enrich a performance, *not* to become crutches for the actors. Too often, amateur productions and actors rely on props to shore up their weaknesses. But a crutch, no matter what shape, colour or degree of beauty it takes on, is still a crutch and will draw attention to itself.

A classic example of using a prop as a crutch is the young actor who always uses a cane when portraying an elderly person. Of all the elderly people you know, how many use a cane? Not as many as our 'stage' elderly, that's for sure. Yet we allow ourselves to be convinced that this prop will strengthen our character portrayal. On the contrary, the audience will probably be more likely to notice the cane than to believe that your actor truly is old.

As a director, you should ask yourself: is a *cane* what makes a person old? Of course not. It's his posture, the length and rhythm of his step, his clothing, his style of speech, and numerous unique actions that make him what he is. A cane in the hand of the actor no more makes him *old* than sitting at a piano makes him a pianist.

When it comes to props, it is always worth asking: is this prop necessary? If the answer is in the affirmative, the first place to look for just about anything you'll need (barring the very unusual) is your local charity shop like Oxfam. Even the smallest of towns often has a shop where used items may be purchased inexpensively.

These shops are also great places to find many of the costumes you'll need. Make your costumes as realistic as possible so your characters will be believable. Beware of stereotypes. Not all grandmothers wear shawls, not all little boys wear shorts, not all little girls wear ribbons and ruffles, not all ill people wear hospital gowns, not all athletes wear warm-up suits.

Be creative as you choose an appropriate costume. The best way to do this is to *observe*. Look at people who are similar to the characters in your production. Glance through magazines and books, watch films or television. When you find ideas, write them down. From these ideas, create a costume that is right for the character.

If you are looking for detailed costumes, check your Yellow Pages or topical directory. However, don't overlook the possibility of having your actors search their wardrobes – or that a good seamstress is quietly hiding somewhere in your organisation or church. Distribute a 'costumes needed' list to your organisation, church, school or family and friends of your members. Always look internally first to fulfil any production needs you may have. This will not only help to cut financial corners, but will involve people in what may prove to be a meaningful and fun experience. It's amazing the number of people who are simply waiting to be asked.

Another option for finding costumes is to work out an exchange with a local clothing shop. The management may lend you the costume in exchange for an acknowledgement or advertisement in your production's programme.

Here are some questions to consider when acquiring props and costumes:

1. To make our production the best it can be, what set props do we need, if any? Rugs? Sofas? Curtains? Backdrops?
2. If we need backdrops to represent certain scenes, who will make them? What materials are necessary? Boards? Paint? Brushes? Can we recruit carpenters from church to help? Can we use people who didn't receive an acting part, but who are skilled in painting and design?
3. Where can we get the set props? Should we put out a request to our group sponsor or congregation?
4. What trim props will we need? Pictures? Lamps? Where can we get them? From the actors? Our group sponsors?
5. What hand props are needed? Books? Pots and pans? Torches? Telephones?
6. What costumes would be the most believable for

each character? Who will need spectacles? Hats/ Coats/Trousers? Dresses? Handbags? What type of shoes?

7. Will each person need more than one change of costume for the production? If so, what changes are necessary? Can the changes be done simply and quickly?

8. Where can we get the costumes? At home? From friends? Charity shops?

9. Do we have a budget for props and costumes? If so, what can we afford?

Finally, and above all else, will the costumes and props enrich and enhance the production? If they won't add quality to your production, don't use them.

Make-up

Apart from bad acting, few things are worse than bad make-up. Doubtless you've seen it for yourself... the young person who looks every bit his age, hair made 'grey' with baby powder and hair spray, dark, furrowed brow lines on his forehead and jowl lines on his lower cheek courtesy of someone's magic marker, and a dusting to give that elderly 'ashen' look. But instead of an 'old person', you wind up with something that looks more like the *Creature from the Black Lagoon*.

A few simple rules of make-up will help.

1. As with other aspects of your production, keep it simple. Start by using simple base make-up: a foundation on the skin, eyeliner on the eyes, blusher on the cheeks, a touch of colour on the lips, and light powder to ward off shine. This will add colour to your actors' faces and wash out those unsightly blemishes that'll appear on a well-lit stage and adolescent Hamlets and Ophelias.

2. Use the necessary highlighting sparingly and tastefully. When you use make-up to transform your actor's appearance or age, use your common sense. Look at photos or people you know who are similar to the character. Note how shadows fall on their eyes, cheekbones, and foreheads. Also note their necks and hands (don't simply apply make-up to the face and stop at the chin, assume most of the skin will be seen by the audience). Practise and experiment with make-up as much as time allows. Always strive for character-enhancing make-up.

3. Always check the make-up under the lights you'll use for the performance – even if they're everyday lights. Often the look you'll get in the make-up area or bathroom *isn't* what you'll see on stage. When the actors think they've perfected their make-up, ask them, one at a time, to stand on stage under the lights you'll use for the performance. Have the others sit in the audience and criticise the make-up. Is it realistic? Does the face contain the appropriate amount of colour? Are the eyes well-defined? Are the neck and hands covered as well? What needs to be changed? Then make any necessary changes in make-up so the characters are as believable as possible.

Say that again?

Now let's turn our ears to *sound*. You may have found the greatest script and the perfect actors and the best props and most ingenious make-up, but if the people in the audience can't hear anything, then you may as well stop right where you are.

I've already talked about the director's and actors' role in being heard by the audience, but there may be more to it than that. Many school auditoriums and church buildings weren't designed by people who thought twice about hearing from a stage. This is an area that is often the least obvious, yet the most important. Good, audible voice amplification is critical to *all* productions no matter how simple or complex. Very few buildings have natural acoustics good enough to play without amplification. If someone tells you their building has perfectly natural acoustics, they probably mean that a shouting preacher or a 200-year-old pipe organ can hold its own in the room. These sort of 'natural acoustics' won't be very helpful for most productions. A good sound system is a vital for any audience over fifty people – though I highly recommend it for *any* size crowd, if you can.

I can't make any specific recommendations on types of speakers, mixing boards, or amplifiers. Those decisions depend on your venue and your budget. Like I mentioned about costumes, you may be able to borrow equipment from a local company in exchange for credit in the printed programme. Or sometimes companies will lend the equipment to non-profit productions as part of their community service outreach.

If your venue already has a sound system, you may be inclined to breathe a sigh of relief. I wouldn't. At least, not until you've checked it over to make sure it's appropriate for your production.

For example, can it handle the number of microphones you'll need for all your actors? (This may be the point when you begin to laugh... and can't stop until the end of the chapter. Sound and lights may be completely outside of your scope. But I'll explore them anyway.)

Microphones
There are one or two things you should know about microphones.

1. If it's at all financially possible, the best type of microphone for stage is a remote cordless system. These remote systems require no microphone cable and give the actor complete freedom of movement on stage. In addition, the cordless lapel microphone is very small and can be hidden easily without impeding the sound quality or amplification. The transmitter for the microphone is generally small enough to be hidden on a belt under the actor's clothing. One major drawback to the use of a remote sound system is cost. If ever there was a product that holds true to the adage 'you get what you pay for', it's a remote system. Some systems may be reasonably priced, but experience has shown that the less expensive systems don't sound as good and may even pick up local radio stations on certain frequencies ('To be or not to be... and now for today's weather... ') The use of batteries can also become a major expenditure. The average alkaline battery life on a normal system is a maximum of four hours. If you have a number of microphones and do numerous performances, this will add up. (If you use a remote system for your production, always have someone check that all microphones have fresh batteries, that all receivers are plugged in, and that everything tests as it should. In other words: do a sound check! Also, be sure to rehearse the use of remote microphones with your actors – on and off stage – to avoid any embarrassing moments when an actor has gone off-stage and begins to talk to someone there.)

2. The alternative to a remote system is to use normal microphones on stands. Here are a few tips to keep in mind if you have to do this:

- Always make sure that the microphones are placed slightly *below* the mouth at an approximate 45-degree angle. This will allow for maximum pickup (gain) and lessen the chance of feedback. When setting the height, do so in a comfortable stance – not unnaturally erect or slouched.
- When positioning a microphone, depending on where the dialogue takes place, put the microphone in favour of your performer's right or left. For example, if the actor is seated or standing and is talking to someone on her right, have her positioned slightly to the left of the microphone. Proper positions will determine how well the actors are heard. Obviously, if a monologue is delivered to the audience, then the microphone should be centred with the mouth.

3. Always set up your microphones before the production starts, and only move them during a blackout. Don't let your performers fiddle with them, lean on them, or even look at them. If you give the visual idea that the microphones don't exist, the audience won't notice them as much. If for some reason a microphone must be moved or adjusted, do so without looking at it: reposition it quickly and fluidly. Only do this when you are already moving on stage and during someone else's lines. Co-ordinate such movement with your sound person so he or she will know to turn that particular microphone off before it is moved. We are all aware of the annoying crash, bang and boom that accompany moving a microphone.
4. Be careful of microphone cords. Be aware of the position of cords so as not to trip over them. After a microphone is in position, always shake out any

tangles in the cord, then pull it to the microphone stand so that it doesn't drape out and away from the stand.

Whatever sound equipment you use, it's wise to rehearse with your actors and the equipment as much as possible before the performance.

Let there be lights

Just as sound allows the actors to be heard, light allows them to be seen. Lighting can do more than that if you have the talent and facilities. Even a simple, well-constructed lighting system can turn an average presentation into a more effective performance. Lighting establishes moods. Through very simple colours or combinations of colours (blue=cool, red=warm, etc) you can draw the audience into the right frame of mind for a scene. You can also convey a lot of information to the audience about the setting, the time of day or night, what character or part of the stage they should be focusing on, etc.

Lighting also acts as a visual punctuation mark. When a comedy sketch ends on a punch-line, an immediate blackout serves as an 'exclamation mark' for the humour. Audiences are conditioned for this. When the lights go out, the sketch or scene is over.

For more reflective or pensive endings, a fadeout can be used. This allows for the emotion to carry on for a thoughtful moment or two before moving on to the next sketch or act.

A hint for your actors

When using a lighting system, never move on a blackout or fadeout until the lights are completely down. As a safeguard, have the actors count to three before they move. Otherwise, the audience will see them break character or move in a way that has nothing to do with the play. The illusion will be broken. It's no longer a character moving purposefully across the stage but an actor scrambling to get to his next position. It reminds the audience that they're only watching a bunch of actors.

The equipment
Here's a quick overview of a few of the more widely-used lights. You can decide which may be best for you:

- The Fresnel light. This light is very useful because it can be adjusted to cover larger or smaller portions of your stage. It is especially good for down-stage areas if you're hanging the lights from ceiling beams or scaffolding. The distance for this particular light is most effective at eight to ten metres.
- The Ellipsoidal light. This light is good for distances over ten metres and has a very flexible beam (because of how the light is constructed) with an intensity that matches spotlights of higher wattage. It is good for beams or up-stage lighting. It can also be fitted with an iris to allow for varying sizes.
- The Follow spotlight. This is what most of us generically call a 'spotlight' or 'follow spot'. It handles distances from twenty-five to forty metres or more and is constructed to cover large portions of the stage or zero in on a single moving performer. It can be helpful in dramatic productions but is more effective in comedy and musicals.

Set construction
All sorts of factors affect set construction: how simple or elaborate your production is; whether you're performing on a stage where you can pound a few nails into the floor or whether you're in a church where you

can't touch a thing; or if you have the knowledge of carpentry and painting to make a set look good.

Some of the things I've already discussed apply here. If the sets are going to look cheap and will distract from the performance, don't use them. If the set is going to distract from the theme of the sketch or play, don't bother. Inversely, if you think a set is somehow going to make up for deficiencies in your acting, spend the time on your actors instead.

It's a fair guess that you probably won't have the time, budget or manpower to build sets, so I won't delve into the details about tools, timber, canvas, flats, toggle bars, keystones and cross-pieces. If you do want to build sets for your production, then I suggest you seek out a more advanced manual than this to help you along.

Promoting the production

Depending on what kind of production you're doing and who you want to reach, there are a number of good ways to publicise the event. But *first* you must make certain that your outgoing information contains all of the following: *who* is doing it, *what* they're doing, *when* they're doing it, *where* they're doing it, and *how* to get in to see it (through tickets, free admission, donations, etc).

In the organisation

If you're part of a school or church, the first few outlets for publicity are right under your nose: word of mouth; printed announcements in the newsletter, bulletins, or through a mailing; verbal announcements from the pulpit, in assemblies, in the various classes and activities.

In printed material, make sure your production stands out from other events by looking stylish and appropriate to your production. You may even consider doing a sketch or portion of the production in church or assembly as a preview of what's coming.

Posters and flyers

Create some nice, appropriate artwork or photos of the cast and put together a variety of posters and flyers. Next to word of mouth, this is the oldest form of publicity. Put them wherever the law allows: in shop windows, on fences, telephone or light poles, signs, community notice boards, etc. Flyers can be handed out in the usual places where people gather and can be very effective for reaching people outside your normal circles.

One note: don't let your posters or flyers become part of the litter problem. After your production has ended, make sure you go back to where the flyers were posted and dispose of them properly.

Press releases and articles

Most local newspapers will accept press releases and articles about your production. They might not *use* them, but they'll accept them. Sometimes they'll take them 'as is'. Other times a reporter may rewrite them. What have you got to lose?

Whenever possible, include a close-up photo of an interesting portion of the show being acted out. This will make your press release look more respectable and increase the chances of it being published.

Apart from an article, most local newspapers have sections dedicated to free publicity for local events. Phone for information about the format and send it in! Many communities also have 'shoppers' guides' with free publicity for non-profit organisations. Ask around, maybe they can help you.

If you have the money, you can always buy

advertising space (often at a discount if you're a non-profit-making organisation).

Radio spots
Most local radio stations allow time for public service announcements for civic and religious groups. Phone your local stations to find out how to promote your production on the air.

Other organisations
Don't forget to send a personal letter describing your production (along with posters and flyers) to other organisations and churches in your area. They're often the ones most interested in what you're doing and often the ones we forget to contact.

A printed programme
The idea behind printing a programme for your performance is, primarily, to let your audience in on what they're about to see and clarify any advance information they may need to follow your production: time, setting, chronology of scenes, etc.

It's also the opportunity to give credit where credit is due. List the name of the play, the author, the players, director, producer, music director, light technicians, sound personnel, and anyone and everyone who contributed to the production. (Don't forget the people who provided refreshments or took care of the nursery for you!) You should also make certain to thank any people or businesses who provided you with props, set pieces, or *anything* that helped with the production.

One small note: never assume you know how to spell someone's name. Be sure to check all name spellings several times *before and after* it has been typed (or typeset). You wouldn't want to hurt or offend anyone who has contributed to your production.

A checklist

To map out your time more effectively, here's a
suggested checklist for your publicity campaign...

Six To Eight Weeks Prior To Your Production:
- Notify any monthly periodicals (local publications,
  magazines, etc).
- Have posters and flyers printed.

Two To Three Weeks Prior To Production:
- Send posters and flyers with cover letter to other
  area organisations.
- Send press releases to local newspapers and
  shoppers' guides.
- Flyers in church bulletins on two or three
  consecutive Sundays.
- Send public service announcements to local radio
  stations.
- Place posters or flyers on community notice boards:
  banks, libraries, shopping centres, etc.
- Contact local bookshops for placement of posters.
  Ask to consider using your flyers as 'shopping bag
  stuffers'.
- 'V.I.P.' invitation list: special invitation to church and
  community leaders who might not otherwise attend.
- Assemble and print your programme.

Ten To Fourteen Days Prior To Production:
- Begin concentrated poster distribution and display
  wherever you can put them.
- Have your group personally distribute flyers around
  the city at shopping centres, in individual shops,
  etc.
- Consider placing a banner or lighted sign in front of
  your church (or place of performance) announcing
  production.

Chapter Eight: Rehearsals: from script to performance

Rehearsals are the means through which you get your actors from mere script-readers to living breathing characters in a world that integrates costumes, make-up, props, technical equipment and all the other components of live theatre. All the pieces are there, rehearsal allows you to assemble them.

We've only just begun...

Figuring out when and how to schedule rehearsals will depend on the difficulty of the material; the experience of your cast; the availability of your rehearsal space; competing activities; and how often the members of your cast can rehearse.

The best thing to do first – and remain fixed to it – is to determine when your opening night is and then work back from there.

Remember: this isn't the West End. It may seem like you should plan for six weeks with five rehearsals each week, but that might not be practical for your group. That's a lot of commitment for a group of unpaid amateurs. (But if they *want* to do it, then go ahead!)

However, you'll need to have a good number of rehearsals to compensate for the lack of experience. Schedule them close enough together to gain momentum: so that directions, characterisation and memorised dialogue will be reinforced from rehearsal to rehearsal. Also, run each rehearsal for at least two hours (and schedule it fifteen minutes *before* you really plan to start – that's the magic amount of time for lateness in classes, meetings, and church services).

But before you rehearse, there are a few things you must do:

1. Reaffirm your goals and plans, and know how you want to carry them out.
2. Know exactly what you're going to do – who will be involved in what acts, scenes or sketches – so you'll use time efficiently. Never go into a rehearsal unprepared. If you do, it'll be a waste of time. Your cast will know it and you'll know it.
3. Hand out an entire schedule for rehearsals – dates, times and places. Indicate which characters you'll be rehearsing with and at what times.
4. Know the material thoroughly. If you don't, the pressure of rehearsal will master you rather than the other way around.
5. Make sure you have all the material you need – scripts, marking pens, schedules, etc.
6. Maintain a balanced frame of mind, one that will push to get things accomplished but also leave room for creative expression and input from your cast.
7. Be realistic in your expectations and articulate deadlines to the cast (for example, when lines should be memorised, etc).
8. Prepare alternative plans for absenteeism and conflicting schedules.
9. Be prompt for all rehearsals. Arrive early enough to set everything up so you can begin when your cast arrives.

10. Don't assume anyone knows anything. Tell all cast and crew every possible detail.

An overview

Here's a very general rehearsal schedule for determining how much time you'll need between the first rehearsal and opening night.

The first few rehearsals should include general goals and plans for the production (or group), reading of the material with discussion and analysis about the material's content, characters, interpretation, and the director's overall views and intentions. This is also the time to show set designs, costume ideas, and sound and lighting plans. But please be careful. Don't overwhelm your cast with too much in the very first rehearsal. Many directors have the tendency, from genuine enthusiasm, to unload *everything* they want to do in the first five minutes of the first rehearsal. That wouldn't be so bad if the cast felt the same enthusiasm. Unfortunately, the cast usually winds up feeling overwhelmed. Don't make your goals bigger than they really are. Remember to take it a little at a time – for their sake and yours.

The next few rehearsals should cover the blocking of the material, divided as needed by acts, scenes, or individual sketches (depending on what kind of material you're using). Here's where your actors will write notes of stage movements, character specifics, line delivery and other acting considerations about the material. This is the development process for what will ultimately become the production seen by your audience. Don't expect too much from your actors since they'll be concentrating on getting the basics down before they can work on any polish. On larger productions, don't expect your cast to do any memorisation until you've done blocking and clarified basic delivery. The reason for this is simple: action will help reinforce the dialogue when your actor is trying to memorise.

In the next few rehearsals continue work on blocking along with development of characterisation, line delivery and general movement (going over it at least twice each rehearsal), bringing together the acts, scenes, or sketches. This is the time when actors should be memorising their parts and begin to work on more character details and polish, bringing the production closer to the opening night performance.

The next 'section' of rehearsals involves running through the cumulative material – acts, scenes, or sketches – incorporating everything you've done up to this point *without scripts* and with as few interruptions as possible. Take time for individual rehearsals for those parts that need more attention.

You should also run through the production with the technical crew (without the actors) to ensure smooth-running dress rehearsals. Though you should be talking to those in charge of costumes, make-up and props on a regular basis, now is the time to make sure everything is coming together as planned.

Your rehearsals should now be more refined, with you and your actors concentrating on areas of polish. You should be able to run through all the material – now incorporating costumes, technical elements, and anything else beyond previous rehearsals. Hopefully, you're now ready for...

The First Dress Rehearsal. Have the actors go through the entire presentation as if you are performing for your audience – making sure everyone and everything is as it should be. Don't forget to rehearse curtain calls! Interruptions should occur only if absolutely necessary. Make notes of problems, but wait until the end of the run-through before you mention the problems and get them corrected.

The Second Dress Rehearsal. Again, the production should be run as if you are performing for your audience (and it's not a bad idea to have people in attendance). Continue working out any bugs in the production, answer any lingering questions, and sort out forgotten details.

The Third Dress Rehearsal. This should be it – everyone and everything are now exactly as if you were doing the Opening Night.

A ten-week rehearsal plan

This is a more specific rehearsal schedule, based on a ten-week rehearsal time.

Week one:
- Review rehearsal schedule and general production goals.
- Read through material as a group. Discuss, analyse and interpret contents and characters.
- Ask actors to read the script more thoroughly on their own.

Week two:
- Discuss basic needs for sets, costumes and props.
- Begin work on characterisation and line delivery.

Week three:
- Begin basic blocking. Have actors take notes on specific movements for their characters.
- Continue work on characterisation and line delivery. Stress the need for memorising lines.

Week four:
- Continue polishing blocking, characterisation and line delivery.
- Have actors begin experimenting with make-up.

- Incorporate props as you acquire them.
- Work on making or borrowing sets and costumes.

Week five:
- Include technical crew in rehearsal. Work on lights and sound.
- Continue developing and polishing blocking, line delivery, interaction with and reaction to other characters.
- Most lines should be memorised.

Week six:
- Individual rehearsals for those parts of the production that need more attention: individual actors, technical aspects, etc.
- Continue polishing all material.

Week seven:
- Rough run-through of entire material incorporating everything you've done. Limit the interruptions.
- Keep experimenting with make-up. See what it looks like under the stage lights.
- All lines should be memorised.

Week eight:
- First dress rehearsal. Run through entire production, complete with make-up, costumes, props, sets, lighting and sound.
- Practise scene changes and movement of microphones. Remember to make the changes smoothly and quietly. Keep the stage area clean.
- Practise covering for each other's mistakes.

Week nine:
- Second dress rehearsal. Run through production, continuing to work out any problems.

Week ten:
- Third dress rehearsal. Final chance for polishing all aspects of the performance. Everything should run smoothly now. Don't forget to practise the final curtain call.

A specific rehearsal schedule

Regardless of what you're planning to work on, here's a suggested schedule of what to do with the time in your rehearsals:

- Start with announcements. Then get everyone warmed up through acting exercises. Review what's been done in previous rehearsals.
- Concentrate on new material to be learned. Take a short break.
- After the break, review what you've just done and then move into more detailed areas of practice – with individual actors or scenes that might need intricate work. For those actors not working with you on a scene or who might be waiting for their time to come up, encourage them to spend the time learning lines or working on characterisation.

Dealing with your actors

Even after you've done everything you can to select the right people with the right chemistry, you're still going to have some problems. Here are a few of the types of people you may encounter as your rehearsals go on...

The Power Strugglers

Almost every cast will have one or two members who will try to take over in some very subtle (and sometimes not-so-subtle) ways. They will automatically tell the other actors where to pick up their lines or tell them what to do. Sometimes they'll tell *you* what to do.

If you see this happening, *privately* explain to them
that you appreciate their help but would like them to
relax a little. You *are* supposed to be in charge, after all.

The 'I can't do it' People

These are the people who can't do it because of
shyness, self-consciousness, overall inhibitions, or even
moral conflict. Be patient and reassuring in public and
then, if you have to, discuss it more thoroughly in
private. Work towards a reasonable solution. If the
attitude continues, gently warn them that you may
have to get someone else to do the part.

The 'I need to try it this way' People

Sometimes you'll have actors who'll want to spend
hours trying and re-trying different things. Given half
the chance, they'll monopolise entire rehearsals while
searching for the perfect way to say a line or explore a
character. Keep a tight reign on that. Nothing could be
more boring or disruptive for the rest of the cast than
to watch the director and an actor beat a rehearsal to
death with a pretentious stick.

The Shysters

These are the people who are painfully shy, but for one
reason or another try out for your production. Know in
advance that they'll need a lot of encouragement and a
lot of your time to warm up to the idea of going on
stage. You can help extremely shy people best by
working with them one-on-one. Ask them to come
twenty minutes early to each rehearsal for extra
coaching. You can also work with them within the
group doing improvisations and exercises. Though you
should be warned: your time and energy may not pay
off. It is possible that you'll get to the opening

performance and they'll freeze up – either before or after they've gone on stage.

The 'Hams'

Naturally exuberant and lively in the spotlight, these people show no fear or inhibition. However, you have to guard against focusing too much attention on the 'hams' and too little attention on the ones who are more quiet, shy or reserved.

When it comes to these types and the other actors you'll be dealing with, here are a few suggestions to consider.

- Remain sensitive to the egos and personalities involved in your production. Few activities will make a person more insecure or vulnerable than the process of getting up in front of a bunch of people and acting – unless they're 'hams' by nature. Problems or confrontations should be handled sensitively and privately.
- Encourage individuals as much as possible and never assume that they know they're doing a good job. Keep telling them. This doesn't mean flatter indiscriminately or lie just to make someone feel good. Your comments must be constructive without being condescending.
- Encourage the group as a whole. Work towards a family unity so everyone will feel like they're playing an important part no matter how small it may be. Possibly help them develop relationships with each other by doing social activities beyond just the rehearsing.
- Make sure you're communicating in terms the cast will understand. Work with them to ensure that they're hearing and understanding you correctly.

- Help your actors maintain their character and sense of emotion by limiting interruptions and distractions, and keeping unnecessary people out of rehearsals.
- As honest as you want to be with your cast and crew, never reveal your own doubts and fears about the success of the production or the abilities of anyone involved. You can do incredible damage by letting a passing comment or feeling slip to the wrong person.
- If you have access to a video camera and player, bring them in for a couple of rehearsals. Videotape troublespots and then let the cast see themselves in action. It can be very enlightening. Suddenly all the things you've been telling them will make sense because *they're seeing themselves* do it. Don't rely on this too much, though. It could actually damage performances and diminish the intuitive role of the director (as more than just the audience's eyes, but their hearts, as well).
- Whatever your cast practises in rehearsal, know that it'll wind up in the performance. If you let mistakes go by consistently, those same mistakes will haunt you when they perform. That's why you have to practise *everything*. For example, if you're working on a comedy, *practise* the pauses where you expect the laughs to occur. This is an easy thing to forget since the funny lines seem to become less funny the more you rehearse them. Have your actors *hold* for the laughs. Tell them, yes, it feels awkward to hold still or remain silent while the audience is rolling in the aisles, but, *for the audience*, time has stood still. Practise it.
- Work towards a perfect performance but *practise* for reality. Your actors must know what to do and how to respond if a line is forgotten or dropped. They

must know how to stay in character and even ad lib,
if necessary, to get the show back on track. The
natural thing for most people is to panic, exclaim
something completely out of character ('whoops!' or
'I forgot something' or 'you missed a line') or freeze
up completely. The goal to impress upon them is to
*keep the audience from realising that something has gone
wrong.* They must *practise* covering for each other's
mistakes. This goal can be practised during dress
rehearsals when they should be proceeding as if
they're in front of an audience. If someone messes
up and doesn't cover well – tell them so. Ask them
how they will handle it if it happens in the real
performance and then guide them to some possible
alternatives. For example, they can cover an actor's
forgotten line by saying the next line with moderate
adaptation.

Key rules for the dress rehearsals

Dress rehearsals should be as close to the opening
performance as possible. This means that the director
must maintain control in the midst of last-minute
insanity. Try to keep an environment that shelters your
actors from the noise and confusion of the task at
hand. Plan to keep all distractions to an absolute
minimum. Limit interruptions to only those things
that bring the rehearsal to a halt (like the stage
catching fire, a broken limb, that sort of thing). And
though every pore in your body will want to stop the
rehearsal to correct mistakes, it's best to resist and give
extensive notes to the appropriate people later.

The dress rehearsal is also the best time to go over
some very basic rules of performance etiquette that,
coincidentally, I'm about to give *you*.

Basic rules of performance etiquette

1. 'The show must go on' – an over-used expression, yes, but still a true one. There are no valid excuses for missing a performance.
2. Treat every performance as if it is the only one and every audience as if they were the most important audience you'll ever have – no matter how small or large. And if a problem arises, never break out of character or let the audience know that there is a problem.
3. Be ready to go on stage at least one hour before the performance.
4. Never leave the hearing range of the stage during a performance unless you are not going on again for the rest of the night.
5. No peeking. It is very unprofessional to peek out front or through stage scenery to look at the audience. Also, keep any distracting back-stage lights or noises from the audience, particularly talking.
6. Don't ever wander through the audience with your make-up or costume on, unless you're planning to stay *in* character. Otherwise, it will destroy the illusion that you're trying to create.
7. The cast must respect members of the technical crew and stay out of their way so they can do their jobs – the success of the performance depends on it.
8. The crew must respect members of the cast and not distract them from concentrating, maintaining their characters, or establishing emotions – the success of the performance depends on it.
9. Personal problems or squabbles have no place back-stage or on-stage. Take them somewhere else *after* the production is finished.
10. Make sure you have a clear understanding of your

responsibilities for the first performance and for subsequent performances.

The first performance arrives

Already?

Okay, quick... go over the mental checklist...

- The programmes are printed, the ushers are in place, the nurseries have a good supply of clean nappies, the tickets are sold or the offering plates are dusted off, refreshments have been prepared for intermission.
- The props are in place, lights are working (bulbs are changed with extras ready just in case), sound is checking out as it should. Though you might be tempted, stay away from any last-minute fiddling with the technical elements – it'll make your crew nervous.
- The cast should be ready to go on stage at least an hour before the production starts (Rule 3 of Performance Etiquette) and *in place* five minutes before it starts. Go back-stage and say a few encouraging words with the cast. Remind them of any problem areas or last-minute titbits (like projecting to the back of the audience and holding for laughs). Assure them of your confidence in their abilities... and never *ever* let on that you're scared out of your wits. (For ongoing performances, this will become a reminder that you're there, a pep talk to help keep the energy up, and a few reminders about polish and tying up loose ends you saw in the previous night's show. Beware of the sloppiness and carelessness that sometimes follows performances after they first open.)
- Everything is ready. Now go somewhere and sit down or pace in the back or whatever it is you have

to do. The success of the production is out of your hands.

A word about those 'last-minute, gotta perform them in five days' sketches

All of the principles we've discussed here apply to a last-minute sketch. Only you've got a week rather than ten to pull the sketch together. This means you need dedicated people who are willing to meet at every opportunity, memorising the sketch while you walk them through the blocking. Your 'Dress Rehearsal' would be the night before the performance, with final rehearsals leading up to the performance itself.

If this isn't possible, you may want to consider doing the sketch in a Reader's Theatre style, with the actors holding their scripts. You still need to rehearse it like any other sketch, since the actors will be acting and *not* reading, but it may prove helpful for those who can't memorise quickly.

Chapter Nine: How did you do?

Apart from the sudden and obligatory emotional collapse that often occurs after the final curtain has gone down, there are still some things you have yet to do.

First and foremost, tell the cast and crew what a good job you think they did – verbally and, if you have the time, through hand-written notes. Save any constructive criticism for another, more appropriate time.

Second, evaluate with your technical directors and your sponsors the effectiveness of your production. (Give yourself a few days for this so you'll have time to become objective and everyone else will have time to gauge the 'days after' reaction from the audience.)

Complimenting the cast and crew is easy, evaluating the production requires answering some serious questions.

The serious questions

1. Did you achieve all of the goals you set for yourself, the cast, the crew, and the material? If not, what wasn't achieved? Why or why not?
2. What did you learn from this production that you can apply to future productions?
3. How did the audience respond during the course

of the performance? Did they laugh when they were supposed to? Were they moved emotionally? Were they bored? In what ways did the production succeed with the audience? In what ways did it seem to fail?

4. What kind of post-production comments have you received from those who attended the performance? Were they positive or negative? What kind of comments could be helpful to you for future productions?

5. What kind of attendance did you have? What age group seemed most represented? Were ticket sales or donations any indication of their pleasure or displeasure with the production?

6. Was the material you performed a wise choice? Why or why not? What would you change about what you selected for future productions? What would you look for in future choices?

7. How well did the actors perform? How would you assess the quality of their performances as a whole? How would you assess the quality of their performances as individuals? Now that it's over, who would you use again? Why or why not?

8. Were the technical people competent? If not, what could have been improved? How would you assess the quality of their job as individuals? Would you use them again? Why or why not?

9. How would you evaluate the directing? Could you see elements in the production that could be attributed positively to the director? Negatively? How could those elements be changed for future productions? Did the director accurately capture the meaning of the material? Was there a good balance between message and medium? Were there any glaring directorial mistakes? What was done well that should be considered in the future?

10. If you had to do the whole production over again, what would you do differently?

11. If you're running an ongoing drama group, what have you learned and how will you proceed from here?

These questions and more will come to mind and should be sufficiently scrutinised before another production is undertaken. (Providing your brain will allow you to even *consider* the possibility of another production. Ever.)

But deep in your heart you know it was worth it.

Part Two

Sketches

I have tried to cover a variety of themes and emotions in this collection of sketches. I have also aimed to assemble a cross-section of dramatic 'styles' – straight drama, parody, satire, narrative, monologues and Reader's Theatre – in order to demonstrate the diversity of theatre. Here are a few ways to use these sketches:

- Discussion starters. Use them for virtually any sort of gathering.
- Teaching supplements. Perform a sketch for assemblies, worship, special services or classes.
- Outreach. Use the sketches with puppets, street ministries, coffee houses or other forms of outreach. The sketches are easily adaptable and can be done with minimal props and costumes.
- Just for fun.

Not all of these sketches are age-specific, some are appropriate for older audiences, some for younger. It's up to you to decide which is best for your audience.

So, we'll begin with the 'Short and simple stuff' – fairly quick and easy sketches – and work our way to 'Sketches for the more adventurous'.

Short and Simple stuff

1. A question of love

In which we hear two different perspectives about a relationship that ended.

Theme
Love versus sex.

Characters
Sharon.
Kathy.
Geoff.
Bob.

Setting
A table in a café stage left and a table in a student lounge stage right. Full lights can be used or two spots to highlight each side as the focus of attention falls there.

[Lights up on Sharon and Kathy at a café table on left and Geoff and Bob at student lounge table on right. It should be obvious that they are oblivious to each other – especially since they are in separate locations. Sharon and Kathy are studying. Geoff and Bob are in a conversation.]

KATHY   *[Looks at Sharon for a moment, then speaks]* Are you all right, Sharon?

SHARON   *[Looks up from books]* Sorry?

KATHY   There's something wrong. What's wrong?

SHARON   There's nothing wrong.

KATHY   I know you, Sharon, and there's something bothering you.

SHARON   I'm reading a book. How can you know something's wrong when I'm reading a book?

KATHY   Because you haven't turned the page in ten minutes.

SHARON   *[Looks at book, surprised]* Oh.

KATHY   Is everything all right with Geoff?

SHARON   *[Pause]* No.

[We join Geoff and Bob who are in the middle of their conversation.]

BOB   Wait a minute, Geoff. You're telling me you don't want to see Sharon any more? You broke up?

GEOFF   Yes! Are you deaf? I just said we did, didn't I?

BOB   I don't get it. I thought you two were doing well. You're, like, *the* couple around here. What happened?

GEOFF   I don't know. Something changed. I... I don't
            feel the same.

BOB   *What happened?*

SHARON   We went out last Friday night like we always
            do. It was a normal night. We went out for
            pizza and hung out at the shopping centre
            and –

KATHY   That's a normal night? You broke up out of
            boredom then.

SHARON   Don't make jokes, Kathy.

KATHY   Sorry.

SHARON   Everything was all right until we left for home.
            We went to the Cricket Ground to... to...

KATHY   Play cricket.

SHARON   I thought we were going to talk.

KATHY   Talk? At the Cricket Ground? The only talk
            that happens there is *body* language.

SHARON   But it's been different for me and Geoff. We'd
            really go there to talk. *[Kathy looks at her with
            undaunted disbelief, Sharon catches on]* Really.
            You know how it is at my house. And his two
            brothers are at home. *[Kathy continues to look at
            her sceptically]* Well, we may have done a little
            kissing but he's never tried to... to... *[she lapses
            into an embarrassed, brooding silence].*

KATHY   He tried.

SHARON   *[Slow to acknowledge]* Yes. He did.

GEOFF   How long have we been going out? Nearly six
            months. I told her I loved her. I mean, if two
            people love each other then... There are ways
            to express love, right? I thought we were

thinking the same thing... feeling the same way, you know? I mean, she said once that she liked how I kissed. So we were at the Cricket Ground and, well, I got a little carried away. It's natural. It's normal. I'm only human, right? And... well... *[pause]*

BOB   Well *what?*

GEOFF   She said no.

SHARON   I said I wouldn't do it unless we were married.

KATHY   How did he react?

SHARON   *[Pauses, shrugs]* All right, I thought. He said he wasn't surprised. I think he was a little frustrated but he said he understood. He even agreed that it was the right thing to wait. He said he appreciated my willpower.

KATHY   And that's it? No 'but I love you and want to give myself to you?' or 'if you love me you'll let me?' None of those lines?

SHARON   No. He took me home. I thought everything was fine.

GEOFF   I respect her, Bob, I really do.

BOB   Yeah? Then why'd you break up with her?

GEOFF   See, I got up Saturday morning and – well, I don't know. Somehow it felt different for me. We were supposed to go to the shops that afternoon and I just didn't feel like going. I went anyway. And that's when it happened.

SHARON   He was completely different towards me. I could sense it. He didn't hold my hand or do all the little things I'm used to when we're together. So I asked him what was wrong. He wouldn't say at first and then he... *[Pauses, on the verge of getting upset, regains control]* He told me he didn't think he loved me any more. He said the feelings were gone.

KATHY   What a prat.

GEOFF   What a pain. She started crying and asking me questions like 'Why not?' and that sort of thing and I don't know any of those answers. It just went away. Who am I – an Agony Aunt? I don't know why it went away.

BOB   You don't?

GEOFF   No.

BOB   Maybe it had something to do with what happened on Friday night. Or what *didn't* happen.

GEOFF   Oh, come on. It had nothing to do with that.

KATHY   It had *everything* to do with that! Sharon, open your eyes. He loved you up until Friday night and on Saturday it suddenly disappears? Excuse me, but I don't think love works that way. Not *real* love. 'Prat' is too nice a name. You're better off without him.

SHARON   But... it hurts, Kathy.

KATHY   It will for a while but then it goes away.

SHARON   I don't want to lose him. I... I've been thinking that maybe...

KATHY   No. Don't say it.

SHARON   Maybe that's how to prove it. I should have done what he wanted. I love him, Kathy.

[Kathy stares at her, stunned.]

GEOFF   So, it's over. That's the way it happens

sometimes. It'll be awkward for a while but... we'll get over it. There are plenty of other fish in the aquarium. Maybe next time the love will last.

BOB   Yeah... maybe next time.

Blackout. [Curtain.]

2. The two complainers

In which we see a conversation between an optimist and a pessimist and the role change that eventually takes place between them.

Theme
The infectious nature of bad attitudes.

Characters
Mandy – A pessimist who spends all her time complaining.
David – Has more optimistic outlook until he talks to Mandy.

Setting
Could take place anywhere. A bench or couple of chairs.

[Lights up on Mandy sitting alone with a long face and slumped posture – obviously depressed. David enters energetically and speaks with enthusiasm as he sits down next to Mandy.]

DAVID   Hi, Mandy – all right? Lovely day, isn't it?

MANDY   *[Shrugs]* Eh. I suppose.

DAVID   You *suppose*? It's beautiful out here.

MANDY   If you say so.

DAVID   What's wrong with you?

MANDY   *[Sighs]* Nothing.

DAVID   Are you sure? I mean, you *look* like something's bothering you.

MANDY   I can't help it. It's a look I inherited from my mother.

DAVID   I've seen your mother and she doesn't look like that. Come on, what's wrong?

MANDY   *[Irritated]* There's *nothing* wrong! My parents wouldn't let me go to Bridget's party, that's all!

DAVID   You were lucky to miss it. Someone called in the riot squad to get it under control. I nearly got nicked.

MANDY   You see? Even *you* were there. My parents made me stay home to finish an essay about *Shakespeare*. I hate Shakespeare.

DAVID   I wish my parents made *me* stay home to finish my essay on Francis Bacon. What I handed in this morning was real crap. It's a good thing for you that your parents are –

MANDY   So cruel, that's what they are. And I'll tell you

something else. Since I didn't go to the party, Nigel hung out with Anne. She's such a tease and Nigel's such a pushover, they're probably engaged by now.

DAVID You fancy Nigel? I always thought he was such a loser. You're better off with someone else. *[Trying to be positive]* You know, Mandy, it seems to me –

MANDY Then my sister ripped a big hole in the dress I was going to wear to the disco this Friday night. She got on one end and the dog got on the other and between the two of them... *[She gestures with hands and makes a ripping noise]* I'd like to have both of them put down.

DAVID Yeah, I think I know what you mean.

MANDY Then Diana has been talking about me behind my back again. She says I've been trying to steal Joe away from her. Can you imagine *me* trying to steal *Joe*? *[David nods his head affirmatively until she looks in his direction and then he shakes it negatively]* He's so ugly. And he has those tattoos all over his arms now. *[Shivers]* Disgusting.

DAVID And his teeth. I've never seen so many shades of yellow. Funny, but I used to like him about five minutes ago.

MANDY And while I was walking to school, I got mud all over the sides of my new jeans – so I had to go all the way home and change again which made me late for my first class. Mr Henshaw was obnoxious about it, as usual.

DAVID Mr Henshaw is a pain in the backside.

MANDY *[Looks at him surprised]* Do you really think so?

DAVID   Yeah. I was two days late on a paper once and he knocked a whole grade off it. He can be a real Nazi.

MANDY   A Nazi. Yeah. Right.

DAVID   And this morning I had a flat tyre on my bike. Could I get any money from my Dad for the bus? Not a chance. He lectured me about taking better care of my things.

MANDY   Well... yeah. That's pretty inconsiderate.

DAVID   As if *he* never had a flat tyre in his life. And my Mum's been nagging me about my room. Good grief, it's not like she doesn't have two arms and two legs.

MANDY   She works, doesn't she? She probably gets tired.

DAVID   Tired! Well, who doesn't get tired? By the time I get to my room it's all I can do to take off my clothes for bed, let alone put them away! And then my little sister got hold of the stapler and decided to –

MANDY   *[Interrupting]* David... David...

DAVID   What?

MANDY   I have to leave?

DAVID   You do? Why?

MANDY   No offence, but... your attitude is awful. I'm getting really depressed talking to you. *[She stands and exits indignantly as David deadpans a look of bewilderment to the audience]*

Blackout. [Curtain.]

3. A father and son

In which a father gives his departing son some advice.
[Appropriate for Father's Day.]

Theme
Relationships between fathers and sons.

Characters
The father.
The son.

Setting
Their front porch.

[Son enters with suitcase, sits it down and begins searching pockets for his car keys. Father enters.]

FATHER   Is that the last of it?

SON   *[Gestures to suitcase]* That's it. Now all I have to do is remember what I did with my car keys.

FATHER   Son... before you go... I was wondering if we could have a little talk.

SON   If it's about the birds and the bees, I already know.

FATHER   You do? Who told you?

SON   Mum.

FATHER   But you weren't supposed to know until you were eighteen. I told your mother *explicitly*.

SON   Dad... I'm nineteen.

FATHER   Oh. *[Beat]* That's all right. It's not what I wanted to talk to you about anyway.

SON   All right. I'm listening.

FATHER   You're moving out into the real world, Jimmy, and –

SON   Johnny.

FATHER   Hmm?

SON   Johnny. Jimmy moved out last year.

FATHER   Oh. *[Beat]* I wonder if I had this talk with him, too?

SON   I doubt it. You were away on business when he moved out.

FATHER   That's right, I was. Well, son, you're moving out

into the real world and you've got to be very careful. You're going to meet all kinds of people and get caught up in some very precarious situations.

SON   That already happened in school.

FATHER   It did?

SON   Yes.

FATHER   Where was I?

SON   I think you were working in the garden.

FATHER   Somebody should have come and told me.

SON   We would have but you know how loud the lawnmower is.

FATHER   That's it – I'm buying one of those electric ones.

SON   Was there any other fatherly advice you wanted to give me, Dad?

FATHER   No, I don't suppose so.

SON   Well… thanks, Dad. I'll always remember what you've told me here today. *[Starts to pick up suitcases]*

FATHER   Choices. I was going to say something about choices.

SON   I beg your pardon?

FATHER   When I was getting ready to move out of my house, your grandfather gave me some parting words about choices. He said, 'Son, you're going to have to make choices. Lots of them.'

SON   And what did you say?

FATHER   I said, 'You're right, Dad.' Disagreeing with him could be a time-consuming process.

SON   So you thought you'd carry on the tradition
           and tell me the same thing.

FATHER   Sort of. It has a certain poetic justice to it. See,
           you won't have your mother and me to tell you
           the right way to choose. You'll be on your own.
           Your own man. A small, fragile child lost in a
           giant jungle. A tiny speck –

SON   What are you trying to say, Dad?

FATHER   What am I trying to say? *[Beat, as if trying to
           remember]* What *am* I trying to say? *[Beat]* What
           I'm trying to say is that one choice you must
           make daily is who you're going to serve.

SON   I'm not a waiter, Dad. I work with computers.

FATHER   I'm talking in the spiritual son, sense. *[Corrects
           himself]* The spiritual sense, son. You can serve
           yourself, money, Satan, God, or just about
           anything.

SON   You're right.

FATHER   Even if you decide not to choose, you've made
           a choice. You're always going to serve someone.
           Remember that. I hope your mother and I have
           instilled in you the desire to make the right
           choice.

SON   You have. Don't worry.

FATHER   I'm not worried. Your mother asked me to do
           this.

SON   She did? But she said all this to me last week.

FATHER   Really? You're joking. Why does she keep doing
           that?

SON   Thanks, Dad. It meant a lot more coming from

you. I enjoy these father and son chats. We should do them more often.

FATHER   I *would* – if your mother would stop getting there first.

SON   Well... I have to go. *[Begins searching pockets]* I can't imagine what I did with my – *[pulls out keys]* keys.

FATHER   I'm going to miss you, son.

[There is a moment of silence.]

SON   Do you think we should hug or something?

FATHER   Yeah. Why not?

[They embrace.]

SON   *[Picks up suitcase, moves to exit]* See you later, Dad. Thanks for the advice.

FATHER   Did I really give you any?

SON   Uh huh. And I'll be sure to pass it on to my son, too. See you in three days. *[He moves to exit]*

FATHER   See you later, Jimmy.

SON   Johnny.

FATHER   You, too. *[Beat, realisation]* Three days? What do you mean, 'three days'?

SON   I'm only going away for the weekend. *[Exits]* Bye.

FATHER   *[Confused, speaks after he has gone]* But I rented your room!

Blackout. [Curtain.]

4. The job applicant

In which a young lady puts in an application to become an adult.

Theme
The meaning of adulthood.

Characters
Gowers – The agency representative. Should be dressed very business-like, no-nonsense attitude, yet friendly.
Emily – The applicant. Very caught up in her youthful attitudes.
Loveland – An older gentleman.

Setting
An office [or two chairs representing an office] and a metal rubbish bin.

[Lights up on the office. Mr Gowers is sitting in his chair taking notes on a clipboard. Emily enters. He rises to greet her.]

GOWERS   Come in... *[Looks at clipboard for her name]* Emily. Please sit down.

EMILY   Okay. *[She sits down]* It said in the paper that you could help me.

GOWERS   We'll try. Our motto here at the National Opportunity Agency is: 'Whatever you do, we'll find a spot for you.' Anything at all. It's guaranteed or your money back.

EMILY   You better. I'm getting impatient. I've been at this for at least six years.

GOWERS   What exactly do you want to be?

[During their conversation, he takes notes diligently.]

EMILY   An adult.

GOWERS   *[Pause]* Sorry?

EMILY   An adult. You know: a grown-up. They're the ones who get to do what they want when they want, right? So I want to be an adult.

GOWERS   *[Begins flipping through pages on clipboard]* I don't know if I have a form for that.

EMILY   You said it was guaranteed.

GOWERS   Yes! Yes! Of course it is. But... well, that may be difficult. Everyone wants to be an adult these days – except the adults, of course. They want to be children. Let me get a few preliminary questions out of the way and we'll see. How old are you?

EMILY   Sixteen.

GOWERS   And what kind of qualifications do you have?

EMILY   Qualifications?

GOWERS   Practical experience.

EMILY   You must be joking. I survived puberty, didn't
           I?

GOWERS   Yes. But how have you utilised your experience
           – your youth – to qualify you as an adult? I
           need to hear a few practical highlights.

EMILY   Well... I've learned how to *look* like an adult.
           When I was fifteen I could get into bars and
           restricted films. Don't you think I look like an
           adult?

GOWERS   You certainly do. But I have twelve-year-olds
           who can do that. All children look older these
           days. I need something more substantial.
           More... impressive. What have you done? What
           do you know?

EMILY   Know? I know *a lot*.

GOWERS   For example?

EMILY   I could tell you a few things about retail,
           economics and high finance.

GOWERS   *[Impressed]* Then please do.

EMILY   I use my Mum's credit card at the shops every
           weekend. That's retail, economics and high
           finance, isn't it?

GOWERS   Hm. I suppose. Anything else?

EMILY   *[Thinks about it a moment]* I know about
           anatomy. I can tell you anything you want to
           know about spots and unwanted body hair.

GOWERS   *[Writing]* Anatomy.

EMILY   I can also tell you how many calories are in the chocolate bars and biscuits I eat. And I dissected a frog once without throwing up.

GOWERS   *[Scribbling on his paper]* Right. So you've picked up some practical knowledge in maths and sciences. How about literature and the arts?

EMILY   I read all the latest fashion magazines and I know all the words to the *best* songs. The *cool* stuff – not the rubbish.

GOWERS   *[Writing]* Cool stuff. Any experience in psychology or sociology?

EMILY   I know how to make my parents feel guilty when they punish me. And I know how to get them to buy me make-up and dresses I don't need.

GOWERS   How are you at things like time management?

EMILY   Time management? I know how to walk my younger brother to football, meet my boyfriend at the shops, have fish and chips, see a film, *and* pick up my brother again – and still have time to watch *Neighbours*.

GOWERS   Organisation skills?

EMILY   I can fit everything under my bed so Mum thinks my room is tidy. I'll bet you know a lot of adults who can't do that!

GOWERS   Most adults don't have to. That's what garages are for. Anything else?

EMILY   I know how to skive my classes without my parents finding out. I know how to write essays so it sounds like I know what I'm talking about. And I know how to cheat on my exams without anyone seeing me.

GOWERS   I understand. Do you have any technical skills?

EMILY   I can work my radio, curling iron, telly and telephone all at the same time.

GOWERS   *[Looks]* I have nine-year-olds who can do that. How are you at taking care of yourself? Are you self-sufficient?

EMILY   I know how to stick a sock down my brother's throat when he needs it.

GOWERS   I mean *financially*.

EMILY   I've got my parents convinced that they're failures as parents if they don't give me a lot of money.

GOWERS   I see. Do you have any references?

EMILY   My best friend Barbara will talk to you – if we're still on speaking terms. She's mad at me because John Allison likes me instead of her.

GOWERS   Anybody else?

EMILY   John – he's my boyfriend – he could tell you a lot.

GOWERS   That's what I'm afraid of. Anybody *older*?

EMILY   Nobody older likes me.

GOWERS   Oh. *[Writes a couple of final notes]* Well, Emily, I think that covers all the areas we need. You're looking to be an adult with a background of youth spent on nothing but self-centred pleasure-seeking and blatant manipulation. Is that correct?

EMILY   Sounds good to me.

GOWERS   No promises – but I'll see what I can do. With

a little more experience, I'm sure you'll be an adult in no time.

EMILY   Not too much longer, I hope. I want to hurry up and get out of the house. My parents are driving me around the bend. *[Beat]* Is that it?

GOWERS   *[Stands]* I have all the information I need right here which will go in with the appropriate files. Thank you for coming by. *[Extends hand to shake]*

EMILY   Nails haven't dried. *[Stands]*

GOWERS   Oh. Sorry.

EMILY   No problem. Goodbye. *[She exits]*

GOWERS   Youth have become so specific these days. It'd be nice to hear from someone who just wants to be a fireman or a computer programmer or something easy.

[An older gentleman enters.]

MAN   Mr Gowers?

GOWERS   Ah… *[Checks name on clipboard]* Mr Loveland. What can I do for you? Wait – don't tell me – you want to be President of a company.

MAN   Actually, I want to recapture the lost innocence of my youth. You're guaranteed, right?

[Gowers looks to audience, deadpanned expression.]

Blackout. [Curtain.]

5. The wrong feelings

In which a daughter learns that what she feels doesn't count.

Theme
Feelings and expectations between a mother and
daughter.

Characters
Caroline – The mother.
Julia – The daughter.

Setting
Any room in the house where a mother and daughter
might talk.

[A home. Julia has just come home from school. Caroline enters.]

CAROLINE   Hello, Julia. How was school?

JULIA   *[Shrugs]* It was all right.

CAROLINE   Is something wrong?

JULIA   *[Holds up a stack of books]* Do you see these books?

CAROLINE   What about them?

JULIA   Don't you see the mud? Hannah and her gang knocked them out of my hands. On purpose. *Again.*

CAROLINE   That's too bad. They're juvenile delinquents. You have to ignore them.

JULIA   Ignore them! How can I ignore them when they push me around all the time?

CAROLINE   All the time? Perhaps we should talk to the headmistress, then.

JULIA   That would only make it worse.

CAROLINE   Then I'll talk to their parents myself.

JULIA   What? You can't Mum. I would be embarrassed for life.

CAROLINE   Then what do you want?

JULIA   I want them to leave me alone.

CAROLINE   Have you tried telling them to leave you alone?

JULIA   You don't understand. I can't talk to them. I'd rather go to another school.

CAROLINE   Don't be absurd. You can't go to another school simply because a few girls pick on you. Honestly, Julia. You need to be more assertive. They only pick on you because you don't stand up to them. You're like this with everyone, you know. You're a pushover. Talk to them directly and firmly.

JULIA   I... can't. Don't you understand? I can't! I feel too embarrassed!

CAROLINE   Well, you shouldn't feel that way.

JULIA   But I *do* feel that way, Mum. I can't change my feelings just because you say so!

CAROLINE   If you're not willing to change, then there's nothing *I* can do.

JULIA   You don't always have to *do* anything, Mum. Sometimes all I want is for you to listen... and understand. But I suppose that's asking too much. *[She exits]*

CAROLINE   *[Shrugs]* Daughters. *[She exits]*

Blackout. [Curtain.]

6. On the street interview: Being a man

In which a jogger is asked a question by a reporter.

Theme
Masculinity.

Characters
Jogger.
Interviewer.
Cameraman.

Setting
Somewhere on the street with a bench.

[Jogger comes on stage, huffing and puffing, warming up for his big run. He stops at the bench to go through some rather silly-looking muscle stretching exercises.]

INTERVIEWER Excuse me, sir.

JOGGER *[Nervously]* What?!? What do you want? *[Looks curiously]* Are those cameras? Look, I was found innocent on all charges.

INTERVIEWER We're doing an *On The Street Interview* to find out what you think being a *Man* really is.

[He begins to speak with a nervous lack of confidence, but gets caught up in his own nonsensical speech – leading to a climactic orator's nightmare.]

JOGGER Being a Man? Well… I don't know. It's not something real men like me stop and think about. *[Chuckles nervously, no one else laughs]* Lessee… Being a man is… being in control, being successful, being in shape, being strong and true, being healthy wealthy and wise, being real, being all that you can be when all around you are losing theirs. Being a man is taking the bull by the horns and knowing when to come in out of the rain when you're on the ropes. It's keeping the ball rolling when you have an ace up your sleeve and no arms to hold you. It's cutting right to the chase, getting down to brass tacks, burying the hatchet without jumping the gun behind the eight ball. It's knowing when to fish or cut bait, to go the whole hog, to face the music while the Saints come marching in. A real man knows that a bird in hand is worth two that flock together because the early bird catches the worm. He knows better than to count his chickens before they're hatched after putting all his eggs in one basket. And he never puts the cart before a gift horse in the mouth. When he's up against the wall, he doesn't throw in the towel or cry over spilt milk. No, he tightens his belt because he knows that there's more than one way to skin a cat after it's let out of the bag. That's how the cookie crumbles. A real man keeps his head above water, his eye upon the sparrow, and his money where his mouth is, because when the chips are down he has to take the good with the bad and keep those home fires burning! He's the sum total of his parts. He's a friend indeed to a friend in need, to have and to hold, in sickness and in health, with liberty and justice for all! You ask me what a real man is? He's a – a – *[Looks out, the interviewer and camera are gone]* hello? Anybody there? *[Pause, shrugs, then jogs in place and takes off]*

Blackout. [Curtain.]

7. The environmentalist

In which a stick of gum becomes the centre of an environmental conflict.

Theme
Taking care of the environment.

Characters
Two people of any gender.

Setting
A street.

[A street. First person enters, unwraps a stick of gum and drops the wrapper on the ground. Second person enters immediately – and confrontationally.]

SECOND PERSON   Hey! What do you think you're doing?

FIRST PERSON   Having a stick of gum. Why?

SECOND PERSON   *[Points to the wrapper on the ground]* I'm talking about *that*.

FIRST PERSON   What about it?

SECOND PERSON   It doesn't belong down there – that's 'what about it?'!

FIRST PERSON   Oh yeah? Well, I don't see a rubbish bin anywhere.

SECOND PERSON   So the whole earth becomes one for you? *[Picks up the wrapper and accompanying foil]* You don't want a rubbish bin anyway. You can recycle this, you know. The paper and the foil.

FIRST PERSON   Really?

SECOND PERSON   Absolutely. Do you have any idea how bad the rubbish problem is? The average family throws away about 100 *pounds* of rubbish every week. Do you know how much rubbish you'll throw away in your lifetime? Close to 600 times your adult weight.

FIRST PERSON   That's not so much.

SECOND PERSON   And 14 *billion* pounds of rubbish are dumped into the sea every year.

FIRST PERSON   What do you want *me* to do about it? It's just a stupid gum wrapper.

SECOND PERSON	Dispose of it properly – at a recycling centre. Every little bit helps, you know. If enough people do it, we'll reduce the rubbish and possibly save some trees! That's not so hard is it?
FIRST PERSON	I suppose not. But... where should I put it? I don't want to carry it around all day.
SECOND PERSON	What's wrong with your pocket?
FIRST PERSON	Oh. Nothing, I suppose.
SECOND PERSON	Then – go on.

[First person digs into pocket.]

SECOND PERSON	*[Sees someone offstage, shouts]* Hey, you! That bottle can be recycled! *[He rushes off]*

[The first person pulls out and dumps whole wads of rubbish onto the ground in order to make room for the gum wrapper. Finally, proudly puts it in his pocket.]

FIRST PERSON	There. I'm proud to do what I can. *[He exits]*

Blackout. [Curtain.]

8. The reconciliation

In which two church members meet to work out their problems – whatever they may be.

Theme
Reconciliation.

Characters
Matthew – The accused.
Steve – The accuser.

Setting
It could be anywhere. Two chairs.

Note
This may be adapted for either two males or two females.

[Matthew and Steve enter silently. They sit down. There is a moment of awkward silence.]

MATTHEW   Well?

STEVE   Well what?

MATTHEW   You wanted to see me. Here I am.

STEVE   Yes... well, the Bible says that if we have a grievance with one another then we should go to the person privately and discuss it. That's why I'm here.

MATTHEW   A grievance? You have a grievance with me?

STEVE   *[Stands, paces]* Yes. It's fairly well-known that you hate me.

MATTHEW   *Hate* is a pretty strong word. We've had our disagreements in the past but –

STEVE   You're saying I'm disagreeable?

MATTHEW   Not at all.

STEVE   But I *am* disagreeable. Everyone knows it. I know it.

MATTHEW   Disagreeable isn't the word that comes to mind.

STEVE   You're calling me a liar?

MATTHEW   No, I'm not calling you a liar.

STEVE   Then what *are* you calling me?

MATTHEW   I'm not calling you anything.

STEVE   I'm a nobody, is that what you're saying?

MATTHEW   *[Confused]* Yes... no... I don't know *what* I'm saying.

STEVE   My point exactly. You never know what you're saying.

MATTHEW   But I *do*! At least I did until we started this conversation.

STEVE   Implying that I'm confusing the issue.

MATTHEW   I'm not implying anything.

STEVE   You're saying it outright.

MATTHEW   What?

STEVE   What you just said.

MATTHEW   What did I just say?

STEVE   Don't be coy with me. We should be able to discuss this man-to-man [or: like two intelligent women].

MATTHEW   We're one short.

STEVE   Aha! Now you're being insulting.

MATTHEW   I'm sorry. I couldn't resist.

STEVE   It's too late to apologise. The damage is done.

MATTHEW   *What* damage? I haven't been able to figure out what you're talking about.

STEVE   We've done enough talking. Now is the time for action.

MATTHEW   What kind of action? What are you going to do?

STEVE   More than *you've* done.

MATTHEW   Done about *what*? What was I supposed to do?

STEVE   Well, if *you* don't know, how should I?

MATTHEW   I suppose you wouldn't.

STEVE   Right. *[Pauses, confused]* So... ah... do you forgive me or what?

MATTHEW   I suppose so.

STEVE   What a relief. *[Pause]* It's amazing. Those Bible verses really *do* work, don't they?

MATTHEW   They're what *I* live by.

Blackout. [Curtain.]

9. The crisis

*In which Jilly wants to help a friend with a problem and
Adrian uses a common-sense approach to talk her out of it.*

Theme
Sacrifice and compassion versus 'good sense'.

Characters
Jilly.
Adrian.

Setting
A living room. [A couple of chairs will do – any more
or less is up to you.]

[Adrian is sitting, reading a newspaper while he waits for Jilly. Jilly enters, putting on her coat as she does. She is making a bee-line for the other side of the stage to exit.]

ADRIAN   Jilly – wait a minute.

JILLY   Oh, Adrian. I'm sorry. I didn't know you were here.

ADRIAN   Your Mum didn't tell you?

JILLY   No. And I have to go.

ADRIAN   To where? We're supposed to go to a film.

JILLY   I can't. Honestly. I have to go to Cassie's.

ADRIAN   Cassie?

JILLY   She's really upset.

ADRIAN   About what?

JILLY   Well... she and Bill broke up.

ADRIAN   And she called you?

JILLY   I suppose I was the only one she could think of. *[Moves to exit]* I'm sorry. I'll ring you later.

ADRIAN   Wait a minute, Jilly. I... I don't feel good about this.

JILLY   Why not?

ADRIAN   I mean... are you sure you should get involved? You hardly know Cassie.

JILLY   She was crying. She needs help. *[Turns to leave again]*

ADRIAN   Hold it. Can we talk about this? I think we need to consider the consequences of what you're doing.

JILLY   Consequences? I'm only going over to talk to
             her.

ADRIAN   Yeah, sure, that's what you're doing *tonight* –
             but what will it mean for the future? Hmm?

JILLY   The future?

ADRIAN   You could get dropped right in the middle of
             something very messy. She'll talk to you
             tonight and then Ben –

JILLY   Bill.

ADRIAN   Bill, Ben, whatever – he'll want you to hear
             his side and there you are.

JILLY   *[Pauses to think]* There I am *where*?

ADRIAN   Right in the middle of a no-win situation.
             You'll have both of them crying on your
             shoulder and if they don't get back together,
             they'll blame you for keeping them apart.

JILLY   But what if they get back together?

ADRIAN   Then they'll resent you for interfering. You
             have to think these things through, Jilly.

JILLY   *[Pondering this]* Well... all right. Just so they
             get it worked out. It doesn't matter what they
             think of me.

ADRIAN   And what if she becomes dependent on you?
             She'll cry on your shoulder tonight, but what
             about tomorrow night or the night after that?
             She'll need you more and more and we'll
             never go to the cinema. I've read about such
             things. It's like a domino dependency.

JILLY   Why would she depend on dominoes?

ADRIAN   No, no, no. Her dependency will trigger *more*
             dependency and that won't be healthy for her

or for you… or me. You'll be getting calls at all hours of the night, you'll have to constantly be there for her whenever she needs you. Jilly, if you go over there now you'll become responsible for her. Are you sure you want that sort of responsibility?

JILLY   I hadn't thought about all of that. I only wanted to help her.

ADRIAN   You see? You have to think before you act. Going over to help her tonight could change everything for us – and we don't want that to happen, do we?

JILLY   No. I don't suppose we do.

ADRIAN   There you go. *[He puts his arm around her and begins moving her to exit the other way]* I think you should ring her back and tell her… tell her something's come up and you can't make it. They'll work it out on their own. All right?

JILLY   Well… you're probably right.

ADRIAN   Of course I'm right. It's a good thing I was here.

JILLY   Yes. It could have been pretty bad for me to get involved in someone else's crisis.

ADRIAN   Now – let's go make that phone call and go to the cinema like we planned.

JILLY   Good idea, Adrian. I'm awfully glad I'm going out with such a wise man.

ADRIAN   And don't you forget it.

[They exit.]

Blackout. [Curtain.]

10. A phone call from Elizabeth

In which the mother of John the Baptist decides to give him a ring.

Theme
The difficulty of commitment, duty and calling.

Characters
Elizabeth – should be played as a stereotypical Hebrew mother.

Setting
Elizabeth's living room with a phone. As simple or imaginative as you want to make it.

[As lights come up, Elizabeth is moving to the phone, talking as if conversing with someone she's left off-stage. As she talks, she picks up the phone and dials.]

ELIZABETH   It's getting out of hand, I tell you. Completely out of hand. He's your son, Zacharias, and what do you do? Are you listening to me, Zach? *[No answer]* I didn't think so. I know you can hear me – that old 'deaf because of God' excuse doesn't work with me. You got your hearing back a long time ago...

[Puts receiver to her ear] Hello, John? Son? Yes, it's your mother. Remember me? Elizabeth, the wife of your father. John, John – can we talk? John, it's your lifestyle. Now don't get me wrong, I'm only your mother, and I know you're headstrong, but, John, I'm concerned about this business of living in the desert. Is that healthy? I've got a nice room right here for you and you're out with cactus and scorpions. I ask you. It must take all your money for sun-tan lotions and dust rags. I mean, John, really, what kind of life is that? It can't be very clean... *[Pause]* Oh. You spend a lot of time in the Jordan River. Great. You're trading dust for mud...

John, please, I hear people talk. A fashionable dresser you're not, I know. But... can we talk? Camel's hair and leather belt, John. That's what they're saying... *[Pause]* Oh. It's true. Well, maybe it'll start a trend. Stranger things have happened.

I'm worried about you, John. I really am. The long hair. The beard. People get the wrong idea. Are you healthy? I mean, what are you eating these days?... *[Pause]*

Locusts. What is that – a nickname for some kind of Chinese food?... *[Pause]* Oh. *Real* locusts. You're telling me you're eating insects, John. I'm your mother, how can I be happy about that? Oh, you eat them with *honey*. Well, that makes me feel *much* better...

John, I have to tell you: I'm concerned about the comments you've been making... *[Pauses]* You know the ones – about the King and his wife? You're not being terribly diplomatic... *[Pauses, holds phone away from ear for a second then holds it close again]*

John... John... don't start that fire and brimstone stuff with me. I'm your mother. I changed your nappies before you covered them with camel hair. I'm not asking you to compromise your message. I'm only saying that there are more tactful ways of communicating. Phrases like 'brood of vipers' just doesn't endear one to the populace, if you know what I'm saying. It's not the way to win friends and influence people...

John, are you listening to me?

I'm worried. Forgive a mother for worrying about her only child. But I'm hearing things about the King and... well, he's not very happy with you. And I don't mean mildly annoyed either. Do you understand what I'm saying?...

[Pauses, tone changes, becomes softer] John, listen to me. When you were a child, I knew God had some special things in mind for you but... *[Pause]* John, I'm afraid. *[Pause]* I know about your mission, John. *[Pause]* I know you have to do what

God commands. *[Pause, getting upset]* I
know all about the sins of this generation,
John, but I don't care about this generation.
I care about *you* because you're my son.
You're my miracle, John. *[Long pause]* Yes,
son. *[Pause]* Yes. I won't keep you. *[She
slowly moves the receiver away from her face]* I
love you, John.

[She slowly places the receiver on the cradle and exits.]
Blackout. [Curtain.]

11. Singles

In which two 'Singles' find themselves in an awkward situation.

Theme
Misunderstanding 'single-ness'.

Characters
Liz.
Jeff.
Margaret.

Setting
Margaret's living room.

[Liz enters casually, Jeff follows awkwardly. He watches her for a moment...]

JEFF   I'm really sorry about this.

LIZ   Sorry about what?

JEFF   This whole situation. It's awkward.

LIZ   I'm used to it.

JEFF   They get a little overzealous. It happens all the time.

LIZ   I know. I know. My sister and her husband do the same thing. I get invited to what I *think* will be a casual dinner with them and the next thing I know, I'm being introduced to someone from his office –

JEFF   Or her hair salon –

LIZ   The grocery store –

JEFF   I don't know where they find them.

LIZ   They found *me* at the bank.

JEFF   I'm sorry. I didn't mean to make it sound like that.

LIZ   That's all right.

JEFF   How did they find you?

LIZ   I've been handling their account for the past year. When they invited me for dinner, I thought it was an innocent invitation.

JEFF   Me too.

LIZ   Some married people aren't happy unless everyone else is married too.

JEFF   Misery loves company.

LIZ   Do you mean that?

JEFF   No. *[Beat]* It wouldn't be so bad if they would
           let us talk normally – like now. We can barely
           get a word in edgeways between their
           philosophies about love and the joy of being
           married.

LIZ   They nearly got into a fight about which was
           more important – the commitment of love or
           how he leaves the toilet seat up and she uses
           his razor to shave her legs.

JEFF   *[Chuckles]* That'd be funny. They'll divorce
           over an argument about marital bliss.

LIZ   That wouldn't be funny.

JEFF   *[Stops chuckling immediately]* Of course not.
           [Beat] At least they haven't given us knowing
           glances and called us 'lovebirds' yet. *[Beat]* So
           what do we do?

LIZ   About what?

JEFF   This.

LIZ   I don't know.

JEFF   I hate it. I really do. Lately I've been wanting
           to get married just to get rid of the stigma of
           being single.

LIZ   It's like wearing a scarlet 'S' on my back.

JEFF   Dad keeps asking me when I'm going to find
           a girl and settle down. He thinks I'm
           homosexual.

LIZ   My Mum calls and makes a ticking sound.

JEFF   A ticking sound?

LIZ   *[Makes sound of clock ticking]* You know, the old biological clock ticking away.

JEFF   Tactful.

LIZ   I don't understand what people expect me to do.

JEFF   Lower your expectations to increase your availability. It's a mathematic formula. I've sorted it out.

LIZ   I stopped going to church because I couldn't stand it anymore. When I wanted regular Bible studies, they kept pushing me into the singles' groups.

JEFF   Oh, yes. The church singles route. I've taken it.

LIZ   They have good intentions.

JEFF   Sure they do. But I don't need a church group to remind me that I'm single. It's a... self-indulgent label. I'm *me*. That's it.

LIZ   It's terrible to say, but... last time I went to one of those groups, I looked around and could understand why most of the members are still single.

JEFF   *[Laughs]* It's the one eyeball in the middle of the foreheads. I'll bet they're great people when they're not brooding about it.

LIZ   Probably.

JEFF   You're not so bad.

LIZ   Thank you. Neither are you.

[Margaret enters – sees them, smiles.]

MARGARET   There you are! I was wondering where you

two little lovebirds sneaked off to. Come back into the kitchen! Dessert is ready. *[Exits]*

JEFF   It's gelatine in the shape of a heart.

MARGARET   *[Entering]* Liz, do you like gelatine?

LIZ   Yes. Thank you.

MARGARET   *[Nods, exits again]* Good! Good!

[They look at each other helplessly for a moment. Jeff extends an arm out to Liz. She puts hers through. They exit.]

Blackout. [Curtain.]

12. The Old Testament

In which a Father and Mother give us their thoughts about the Old Testament and their Son asks a silly question.

Theme
Applying the Bible to everyday faith.

Characters
Father – A typical father who unintentionally butchers his Christianity through his lack of knowledge.
Mother – If there is a way to simplify Christian belief to its easiest cliché, this particular mother will do it.
Son – He's at a point in his life where he's searching for a few answers – and none of them are easy.
Daughter – Her interests – in fact, her entire life – lie in avoiding anything deeper than choosing the colour of her nail polish for the day.

Setting
A typical family living room.

[The family enters as they return from church. The Father is carrying the Sunday paper and systematically hands out various sections to various family members as he speaks.]

FATHER   That was a yawner, wasn't it?

MOTHER   The music was nice.

FATHER   I don't know what gets into the Vicar sometimes.

MOTHER   Maybe it's just a phase.

FATHER   I hope so. And I hope it goes quickly. I don't think I can sit through another one of those sermons. It makes me feel like I'm back in school.

DAUGHTER   I lost him after he said to turn in our Bibles to Deuteronomy.

FATHER   Levites, sacrifices, feasts… was it *supposed* to make sense?

MOTHER   He said next week he would cover the design of the temple in Jerusalem.

FATHER   Now *there's* an incentive to go back. I just don't understand. Usually he's so good at making the Bible interesting. Now it's boring.

MOTHER   Write him another letter.

FATHER   No. The last one didn't help any. He kept right on preaching about whatever it was he was preaching. *[Trying to remember]* What was it?

MOTHER   The amputation of sin.

FATHER   *[Thinking about that]* No, it was the… the *imp*utation of sin. Yeah, that's it. Adam and the seed of Abraham and all that nonsense. I wish he'd get back into the New Testament and study some *Christian* issues. They're tough enough to figure out without confusing them with all that Old Testament nonsense.

MOTHER   All I know is that Jesus died for my sins. God said it, I believe it, and that's good enough for me.

FATHER   That's right, darling. *[Beat]* Maybe I *will* write that letter.

SON   *[Who has been pondering all of this quietly]* But why did he have to die?

[Everyone stops. Turns to stare at him.]

FATHER   What did you say?

SON   I was just wondering... I mean... why did Jesus have to die?

FATHER   Don't ask silly questions.

SON   I never understood that part. There are a lot of things I don't understand.

DAUGHTER   Here we go.

SON   I mean, what does dying on a cross have to do with saving us from our sins? What's the connection?

FATHER   It's redemption... you know, propitiation... sanctification... procrastination... the Jewish nation... all of those -ation things.

SON   Yeah? Now can you say that in English?

FATHER   Of course not. The Bible was written in Arabian. What do I look like – a theologian? I'm a Christian.

DAUGHTER   This is too deep for me. I'm going to change clothes.

[She exits.]

SON   It doesn't make sense.

MOTHER   It doesn't have to make sense, son. It's the Bible. God's ways are not our ways.

SON   I know that, but there must be an explanation for some of it. For example, in the Old Testament when God told the Israelites –

FATHER   Whoa now. Remember, son: that's the Old Testament. It has nothing to do with what we believe now.

SON   But... but it's in the same book.

FATHER   So's Revelation but you don't see me trying to figure that out, do you? I never claimed to be the Archbishop of Canticles, you know.

MOTHER   I think you mean the Archbishop of Canterbury, dear.

FATHER   Oh. Right. *[Beat, to son]* You see what I mean? I don't need to know all that to be a good Christian. We know just enough to –

SON   *[Picking up without missing a beat]* – make us dangerous.

FATHER   Make us dangerous. Right. *[Beat]* Wrong. We know just enough to get along.

MOTHER   Don't be disrespectful.

FATHER   Why is that so hard for you? Why do you have to make things so difficult?

SON   Because there has to be more to it than what

we think. I never wanted to believe that being a Christian meant kissing my brains goodbye. The God of the Old Testament is the same as the God of the New Testament, right? There must be a connection between the two. I only want to know what it is. Does it have to be so hard?

MOTHER   *[Suddenly pleased]* Are you telling us you want to become a vicar?

SON   A vicar?

MOTHER   Vicars are the only ones who care about those things. *[Ecstatic]* Oh, Roger, did you hear that? *[She rattles on as the son reacts and the Father speaks his next line]* Oh, that's so exciting. My son is going to become a vicar.

FATHER   What does a theological education cost these days?

SON   Wait. Hold it. I didn't say that. I was only – *[He continues his lines under his mother's rattling and his father's ponderings]*

MOTHER   *[Undaunted]* Wait until I tell your grandparents!

SON   Aw, don't tell Grandma. I was only trying to –

MOTHER   I should ring them right now while we're off-peak. They'll be so proud. *[She exits excitedly]*

SON   Mum, wait. You don't understand. I didn't mean –

FATHER   Does this mean you won't be allowed to get married?

SON   Time out. Hold on. That's not what –

FATHER   Oh yes, those are priests, aren't they?
          Hmmmm. Well, if you're sure it's what you
          want to do, I'll back you one-hundred per
          cent. You know that. *[Pats him on the back
          supportively, speaking as he exits]* I wonder
          what became of the Radio Times? *[Calling]*
          Honey! Have you seen the Radio Times? *[To
          himself as he exits]* There's a match on today.

SON   *[Shrugging]* That's what I get for asking.

[He exits.]

Blackout. [Curtain.]

13. The sit-in

In which a group of teenagers protest the church's 'meaningless curriculum' by staging a sit-in on the church steps.

Theme
Relevance in the church.

Characters
Reverend Lindsey – The long-suffering Reverend.
Dan – The leader of the 'revolution'.
Roslyn – The assistant leader.

Setting
Reverend's Office. At least two chairs. Beyond that, a desk, books, office decorations, etc might be nice but not necessary.

[Reverend Lindsey's office. Dan [wearing sunglasses] and Roslyn enter first, Reverend Lindsey follows.]

REVEREND   *[Gesturing to chairs]* Sit down.

DAN   Getting bossy won't help.

REVEREND   Sit down, *please.* *[Dan sits down]* Where are your manners? You should let the young lady have a seat.

DAN   That's no lady – it's just Roslyn.

[Reverend rolls his eyes and sits down – at his desk, if one is available.]

ROSLYN   That's all right. I've been sitting for quite a while.

REVEREND   All morning. On the front steps of the church. With *fifty* other young people. What do you think you're doing?

DAN   This is a protest. The youth group is revolting.

REVEREND   Some of the parishioners think so.

ROSLYN   We're staging this sit-in to protest the meaningless curriculum we're forced to endure every week in Youth Club. And we're going to *stay* there until our demands are met.

REVEREND   Demands!

ROSLYN   Yeah. Lay it on him, Dan.

DAN   *[Pulls crumpled paper from his back pocket]* The first thing we want is *[reads]* a biology report.

[Reverend and Roslyn look at him confused.]

DAN   *[Embarrassed]* Whoops. Homework. *[Pulls out*

*another piece of paper – very large – that unfolds
down to the floor. Reverend looks incredulously]*
Here it is.

ROSLYN Hurry up. I don't want my seat on the steps
to get cold.

DAN We want a whole new curriculum for Sunday
mornings – something that's relevant to our
daily lives. We're tired of the ancient drivel
we're being taught.

REVEREND For example?

ROSLYN Come on, Reverend, everything we hear is so
outdated. The needs of youth have changed.
We can't relate to the Bible.

REVEREND Then what do you suggest?

DAN Updated materials. It's a whole new
generation you have here. *[Reading again]* We
want classes on mind expansion through
spiritual medication.

ROSLYN Medi*ta*tion, not medi*ca*tion.

DAN Sorry. It was a typo.

ROSLYN Forget the list. We know what we want. We
want classes on human dynamics and
interpersonal communication.

DAN We want a class on the spiritual significance
of Kafka.

REVEREND Who?

DAN We want encounter groups – with mandatory
attendance by the parishioners.

REVEREND An *encounter* group? Would you like a jacuzzi
with that?

DAN   Can you get one?

REVEREND   I'll see what I can do.

ROSLYN   Forget about that. Just get us a Coke machine
              and pizza delivered every Friday night.

REVEREND   Anything else?

DAN   We want... *[Trying to remember, looks to Roslyn,
              then remembers]* Oh yeah, we want housing for
              the poor and food for the needy, too.

ROSLYN   And peace on earth.

DAN   Yeah, peace on earth.

REVEREND   Obviously you've prioritised this list. Is that
              it?

[Dan and Roslyn look at each other.]

DAN   Yeah.

ROSLYN   I think it'll do for now.

DAN   Why? Can *you* think of something we missed?

REVEREND   No.

ROSLYN   So, what's your answer? Do we get what we
              want or do we sit on the steps until we rot?

REVEREND   Let's see... *[Speaks slowly, striving to be
              diplomatic]* Your complaints about relevance
              are justified. Even the church leaders feel that
              we need to do something about that and
              we're meeting to begin work on changes. I
              doubt, however, that anyone will go along
              with your suggested alternatives. I'm not so
              certain how Christian mind expansion and
              encounter groups in a jacuzzi would be.

DAN   *[Standing]* Back to the steps.

REVEREND   Hold on. I'm sure a compromise can be worked out.

ROSLYN   *[To Dan]* I knew he'd say that. Didn't I tell you he'd say that? *[To the Reverend]* What about the rest of the demands?

REVEREND   I'll... I'll have to speak with the church leaders.

ROSLYN   You're giving us the run-around. Back to the steps! *[She turns and marches off]* You had your chance. *[Exits]*

DAN   It's going to get nasty out there. *[Puts sunglasses on with deliberate dramatic movement]* We're talking about some serious sitting! *[Turns, moves to exit]*

REVEREND   Son... *[Dan turns to him]* What should I tell your mother about dinner?

DAN   Aw, *Dad*... this is a protest! I don't have time to eat.

REVEREND   You're right. Never mind.

DAN   *[Pause]* What are we having?

REVEREND   Lasagne.

DAN   Well... go ahead and leave me some. But I can't promise I'll be there. I'm not supposed to eat with the *establishment*.

REVEREND   All right. We'll set a place for Roslyn, too.

DAN   Bye. *[Exits]*

REVEREND   Bye, son. Have a good day. *[Sighs, speaks to himself]* It's tough being the father of a preacher's kid.

Blackout. [Curtain.]

14. The ministers' union

In which we meet a group of clergy trying to form a Union that will look out for their best interests.

Characters
Reverend Smith – The newcomer to this scheme.
Reverend Daniels – The primary spokesperson. He's Reverend of the Church of the Suburbia.
Reverend Wesson – A staunch believer in the Union. Tough, urban approach. He's Reverend of the Metropolitan Church.
Shepherdess Hopper – The Reverend from the First Church of the Liberated Saints. She's polite yet very firm and dogmatic about the Union.

Setting
Reverend Smith's office. Four chairs will do the job but you can elaborate more if you want.

[Lights (curtain) up on Reverend Smith's office. Everyone enters, Reverend Smith is speaking as they do, finds a chair and sits down.]

SMITH   Sorry I don't have a larger office but – it's all I have.

DANIELS   Hopefully this meeting will take care of that.

SMITH   Yes – about that – you have me puzzled. On the phone you said… well, what *did* you say?

DANIELS   Let me get some amenities out of the way first. *[Gestures to appropriate people]* This is Reverend Wesson from the Metropolitan Church. This is Shepherdess Hopper from the First Church of the Liberated Saints. And I am, of course, Reverend Daniels from the Church of the Suburbia.

SMITH   Nice to meet you. Now, what's this all about?

DANIELS   We represent a new coalition to form a union.

SMITH   A union? What kind of union?

DANIELS   A Reverends' Union.

SMITH   A *Reverends'* Union?

HOPPER   Yes, we feel it's time that clergy everywhere have unified backing – to ensure the same basic benefits as workers in any other field or vocation.

SMITH   I don't understand. What would this union do?

WESSON   What *every* union does! Fight for your rights!

SMITH   But I'm a Reverend. I'm not supposed to have any rights.

WESSON   A popular misconception. It's time for a change. Brother Daniels?

DANIELS   *[Pulling paper from coat pocket]* Here's what we're after... as just a sample, of course. *[Begins reading]* The union would guarantee complete health and dental programmes.

SMITH   Health *and* dental?

WESSON   Who wants a Reverend with yellow teeth? Your congregation doesn't.

SMITH   My *wife* certainly doesn't.

HOPPER   How often have you been counselling someone and suddenly became aware of your breath? A dental programme is a necessity for you to be effective as a Reverend.

DANIELS   The union would also negotiate your salary.

SMITH   Salary? You get salaries?

WESSON   And not only a salary but a percentage as well.

DANIELS   It's what we call our 'Great Commission Plan'. You'll get a percentage of the tithes brought in by new members.

SMITH   *[Not comprehending]* A percentage of the tithes.

WESSON   We're talking incentives, Bill. Do you mind if I call you Bill?

SMITH   Not at all. But my name is John.

WESSON   We'd negotiate your salary twice a year –

SMITH   *Twice!*

WESSON   And that doesn't include cost-of-living raises, an expense account and a company – that is, *church* – car.

SMITH   Expense account and car?

DANIELS   British-made, of course. We have other unions to think of.

HOPPER   You see, this isn't a low class union we're talking about. We're in a position to get you four weeks' vacation *minimum* this year, personal days *and* sick days.

WESSON   And your work week will be thirty-five hours at full pay.

DANIELS   With time-and-a-half overtime and double-time on Sundays.

SMITH   *Double*-time on Sundays? But Sundays are my busiest days!

DANIELS   *[Shrugs matter-of-factly]* There you are.

HOPPER   We are also working with various Bible publishing houses for kickbacks.

SMITH   I don't understand. Are you talking about Bibles with the church name on it?

WESSON   We're talking about financial remuneration for endorsements from the pulpit. Use a particular Bible for your sermon, mention the name and publisher, and they'll give you something for the advertising.

DANIELS   As Reverend, you have a lot of influence over the buying habits of your congregation.

WESSON   Who knows where it can go from there? Bibles, commentaries, lexicons... breakfast cereals!

HOPPER   *[Sudden thought]* Oh! You forgot to mention the Mental Health Benefits.

DANIELS   Oh, yes. Under your health benefits you'll get insurance against burn-out and stress-related

health problems. From hospitalisation to a
sanatorium, if necessary. We thought it was a
nice added feature.

SMITH It is. But I don't plan on going crazy.

HOPPER Who does? Part of the beauty of this union is
that it anticipates the worst.

WESSON *[As if adding to the slogan]* But it *gives* you the
best. We're talking guaranteed study and
preparation time for sermons, standard
appointment hours, only *one* middle-of-the-
night emergency per month...

SMITH How can you guarantee that?

WESSON *[Tough confidence]* We're *union.* We have our
ways.

SMITH All right, I'm intrigued by all this. But what if
my church refuses to go along with it?

WESSON *[Very tough]* Just give us the names of the
opposers and we'll take care of it.

*[Daniels and Hopper look at Wesson – surprised at his
indiscretion.]*

SMITH You're joking, of course.

[As Daniels tries to cover for him, Wesson merely shrugs.]

DANIELS Of course. If your church refuses, then we
strike.

SMITH A Reverends' strike.

DANIELS How else?

WESSON We're talking picket lines, press coverage, the
works. See how long this church lasts without
you as Reverend.

SMITH I'm not sure I want to know.

DANIELS   Are you in? We'd love to have you join us.

SMITH   *[Pauses, thinking, then slowly stands – the rest take the hint and do the same]* Well... I'd really like to think about it a while.

WESSON   Pray about it, too.

SMITH   Can I? Will prayer be included in the contract?

DANIELS   We can negotiate for it, if you want.

SMITH   Thanks. I'll get back to you. *[Shakes their hands]* I appreciate your coming by.

HOPPER   Our pleasure. *[They mutter farewells and exit, leaving Reverend Smith alone to contemplate all they've said]*

SMITH   *[Looking around at his office – such as it is]* I could use a larger office. *[He moves across stage in opposite direction as lights fade]*

Blackout. [Curtain.]

15. The three witnesses of Pentecost

In which we hear three separate eye-witness accounts of the day of Pentecost.

Theme
From Acts, chapter two, the power of the Spirit.

Characters
Bartholomew.
Urbanus.
John.

Setting
Just a bare stage.

Note
This somewhat straightforward re-telling of the day of Pentecost can be performed with all three characters on stage at the same time – or in a Reader's Theatre fashion. You can put the characters in period costume, though I know of performances done in contemporary garb (which gave a modern sense of immediacy to the story).

[Full lights on stage. Bartholomew enters and moves to stage right casually as he speaks...]

BARTHOLOMEW   Do I remember it? You must be joking. How could I forget that day? Next to seeing our Lord physically risen from the dead, it was one of the most amazing things I've ever experienced. We were together in Jerusalem – we believers, that is – celebrating the Feast of Weeks. I'm sorry, you probably know it as Pentecost. Jews had come from all over Israel, from all over the *world*, to be there. Anyway, I stray from the point. We were at Mark's, preparing to start off for the day's activities and suddenly it *sounded* like the wind was blowing. It was a violent sound, as if a storm were about to ravage the city, and it filled our ears until I thought they would burst. I looked up and there was fire all around. Not that anything was burning, the fire was simply *hanging* in the air. It was beyond belief. This fire hung there and then slowly divided into smaller flames that moved above our heads. From that point, I... I don't have the words to describe the feeling... the *power*. Yes, I've thought about it a lot since then and I'd say *power* is a good word for it.

[Urbanus enters, moves centre as he speaks.]

URBANUS   I came into town a few days before the feasts began – my wife and myself. Hadn't been to Jerusalem in years. *Years* I tell you. Urbanus is my name, by the way, and I was selling rugs in Corinth back then but decided I hadn't been away for a long time and thought Jerusalem during the Passover would be a grand idea. Yes, I know. Things were a little unsettled there what with the crucifixions and political unrest – but what do I care for such things? I was faithful to the ceremonies and sacrifices, I was a good Jew who worked hard and – can I confess it? – my heart wanted to go to Jerusalem. I'd been everywhere by then, all the big cities, but *that* city... oh, it had soul. So, there I was walking down the street with my wife and we wander right into the middle of this commotion. I thought the Romans were shaking someone up again but it was a group of Galileans standing around shouting at the crowd. Normally, I wouldn't have thought that reason enough to stop. Galileans, as a rule, don't impress me much. They're fairly unsophisticated, if you know what I mean. I figure they're drunk, try to push on. But my wife is tugging at my arm and I realise that *these* Galileans are talking in a variety of different languages. Everyone – no matter where they were from – understood them. As I said, Galileans are fairly unsophisticated. I've known only a few who could complete a sentence in their *own* language let alone someone else's. But there they were and I was stopped in my tracks and then one of them stood out from the rest and spoke with such... such *power* about the prophet Joel and a person called Jesus whom they called the Messiah.

[John enters, moves left as he speaks.]

JOHN

Jesus told us it would happen. During our last meal, before his arrest, he asked the Father to send a Comforter to us. I am John. I was there. And after he arose from the grave, he said we must stay in Jerusalem until we were empowered from on high. None of us were sure what that meant – or what to expect. The *last* thing we would have imagined would be to march into the streets during one of our most holy feasts, preaching in languages we had never learned, risking arrest and possibly death at the hands of those who killed our Master. We who ran at his arrest, cowered at his crucifixion, and doubted his resurrection were proclaiming him in full view of the world without fear or hesitation. Then Peter – oh, that Peter – stood and preached. Loudly and boldly. I knew Peter could be *loud*, but not quite so bold. He repeated Joel's prophecy concerning the outpouring of God's spirit on his people. He proclaimed Jesus as both Messiah and resurrected Lord. He explained that all of them, like us, were guilty of his crucifixion. By the power of the Spirit he spoke and three thousand were added to our number as believers.

URBANUS

My wife and myself were two of that number. The Apostle's words were strong. He charged us all for having crucified the One sent from God. The Messiah. That day we took into our lives this strange new belief – the fulfilment of all we were as Jews. Shortly after that, I moved from Corinth to Rome, taking my faith with me to be shared there. I aided Paul from Tarsus – maybe you've heard of him? – I helped him in his work to start an assembly of believers there.

BARTHOLOMEW   And we devoted ourselves to teaching and to fellowship, to the breaking of bread and to prayer. We were all filled with awe for many wonders and miracles were taking place among us. All of us stayed together and had everything in common as we sold our possessions and goods to give as each had need. And we continued to meet and proclaim Jesus in the temple courts and broke bread in various homes and ate together with glad and sincere hearts, praising God and enjoying the favour of all the people. And the Lord added to our number daily those who were being saved. Have I forgotten anything?

URBANUS   It's all written down in case you did.

JOHN   May the power work in you now as it did for us.

[Nodding their approval, they exit.]

Blackout. [Curtain.]

Sketches for the more adventurous

16. Baby-sitting

In which the perfect opportunity for some snogging becomes a question of trust.

Theme
Trust between parents and their children.

Characters
Katie.
Pete.
Katie's father.
Katie's mother.

Setting
Katie's living room. Three folding chairs can be set up as a couch. Also needed: a folding table with a cloth large enough for Pete to hide under.

[Pete sits on the couch nervously, his right leg pumping furiously. Katie enters.]

KATIE   That's it.

PETE   The brat's asleep?

KATIE   Three bedtime stories later – yes.

PETE   What bedtime stories?

KATIE   *[Sits down next to him]* One 'Curious George', one 'Paddington Bear', and Leviticus.

PETE   Leviticus?

KATIE   It's a book in the Bible. I made it as far as the laws for leprosy and she was *gone*. *[They sit for a moment. Pete's leg still pumping nervously. With comic deliberation, Katie slowly looks at it]* Do you have to go to the toilet?

PETE   No. It's just excess energy. Look, are you *sure* your parents won't mind my being here?

KATIE   Of course they'd mind. But they won't know because they won't be back for hours and they won't suspect because they trust me.

PETE   Oh, good.

[Katie snuggles close to Pete.]

KATIE   So, what do you wanna do?

PETE   I don't know.

[She looks at him a moment with anticipation.]

KATIE   Well?

PETE   Well, what?

KATIE   You know.

[Pete smiles as he puts his arm around her and moves to kiss her – his leg pumping again. She suddenly grabs it to make it stop.]

KATIE   Your leg is driving me crazy! *[Imitates it pumping]* It's like sitting on top of an earthquake.

PETE   *[Crossing his legs tightly]* There!

KATIE   Thank you.

[They lean to kiss again but suddenly Pete sits up, listening.]

PETE   Did you hear that?

KATIE   *[Unalarmed]* What?

PETE   A car! I think I heard a car!

KATIE   A *what*?

PETE   *[Jumping up, racing around, trying to think of a place to hide]* What should I do? Where should I hide?

KATIE   Pete! *[Gets up]* What's wrong with you?

PETE   Your *parents*. I think your parents are home! I heard a car.

KATIE   *[Moves right, looks out the window]* It's not them. Will you relax? *[Sits down]* They went to town for a *show*. They won't be back until after midnight. What's your problem?

PETE   I don't know. *[Sits down]* Coming over while you're baby-sitting makes me

	nervous. *[Leg starts pumping]* It always makes me nervous. You remember what happened last time.
KATIE	Last time?
PETE	Yeah, remember how I had to scramble out of the kitchen window and tore my trousers?
KATIE	*[Sternly]* We've never done this before, Pete.
PETE	Sure we have! Remember? You were watching your brother –
KATIE	I have a sister.
PETE	And then I came – *[Pause, beat, realises his faux pas]* It was a dream I had. You had a little brother and… and… in fact, it was crazy… you had red hair and… and, in fact, you were an entirely different person. Yeah. You know how dreams are. *[Leg is pumping harder]*
KATIE	Pete…
PETE	Yeah?
KATIE	I'm going to break your knee cap if you don't stop shaking your leg.
PETE	*[Stops his leg]* Funny… that's what you said in the dream. *[Stands awkwardly]* Look… maybe I should go home.
KATIE	Maybe you should.
PETE	You want me to go?
KATIE	Good grief – I don't want to give you nightmares.

PETE   I'm being silly and stupid.

KATIE   You're not being *silly*. *[With great clarity]*
               Pete, my parents won't be home for
               hours. Got it?

PETE   *[Sits back down]* Yeah, I suppose. I don't
               know what it is. Maybe it's because my
               parents think I'm at youth club. I'll be all
               right. Forget about it. *[They settle back to
               kiss again and, again, he suddenly sits up]*
               It's this whole *trust* thing. You said your
               parents trust you and my parents trust me
               and here we are.

KATIE   Oh, brother.

PETE   We're talking about *trust*, Katie. Your
               parents. My parents. Us. Without a
               foundation of trust – what do we have?

KATIE   Adolescence.

PETE   Right. *[Beat]* Wrong. We have… we have…
               [Struggling with the idea] families without
               trust. That's what we have.

KATIE   *[Rolls her eyes, sits back]* This is great. I
               want Romeo and I get an Agony Aunt.
               Get to the point, will you? If you don't
               like my kissing, why don't you say so?

PETE   I like your kissing. I like it *a lot*. It's only
               that… well, I'm feeling… *guilty*.

KATIE   Guilty.

PETE   *[Shrugs]* I don't know how to have fun
               without guilt.

KATIE   *[Sighs]* I heard you were like this. I didn't
               want to believe it.

PETE   We're betraying our parents' *trust*, Katie.
                That's the point. If they showed up now,
                you wouldn't feel bad for getting caught,
                you'd feel bad for betraying their trust in
                you.

KATIE   I'd feel bad for getting caught.

PETE   You mean to tell me that if we were
                sitting here just like this and we heard a
                car pull up *[SFX: car pulling up]* just like
                that and the sound of car doors slamming
                [SFX: car doors slamming] just like that –

[They both freeze, suddenly look straight ahead.]

PETE AND KATIE They're home!

*[Panic ensues as they try to decide what to do and, after
several attempts to hide in various spots, Pete finally hides
under the table where we can see him, but Katie's father
can't. Katie tries to look nonchalant as her parents come in.]*

KATIE   Hi! What are you two doing home?

MOTHER   I don't want to talk about it. I'm going up
                to change. *[She exits]*

KATIE   Dad?

FATHER   The tickets are for *tomorrow* night. I can't
                imagine what I was thinking. How was
                everything here?

KATIE   Oh... everything is all right.

FATHER   Good. *[Turns to exit, beat]* Oh. Y'know, I
                noticed... *[Tries to remember name]* oh,
                what's his name? The latest in your long
                line of boyfriends.

*[Pete reacts to his being the 'latest in a long line of
boyfriends' – sitting up and bumping his head against the*

table. Katie covers for him immediately by coughing and slapping the top of the table.]

KATIE   Sorry. Something tickling my throat. You must mean Peter.

FATHER   I suppose. I think that's his bike out front.

KATIE   Really? He... must've parked it there to go to Billy's across the street.

FATHER   I didn't know he and Billy were friends.

KATIE   Yeah, they're... *[she holds up hand with index and middle fingers crossed]* just like that. Very close.

FATHER   Hmmm... *[Turns to exit again]* I never would have put the two of them together as friends. Billy's so intelligent.

[Thud against the table, as Pete reacts to the implication of that statement. Katie repeats earlier cover of pounding and coughing.]

FATHER   You should take something for your throat.

KATIE   I will.

FATHER   Goodnight. Don't stay up too late.

KATIE   *[Nods]* 'Night, Dad.

[He smiles at her, then hugs her.]

FATHER   I know a lot of parents who couldn't leave their daughters home alone to baby-sit. I'm glad we can. Goodnight. *[He exits]*

KATIE   *[Miserably]* Goodnight, Dad.

[She makes sure he's gone. Pete crawls out from under the table as Katie sighs. Pete brushes himself off.]

PETE   Long line of boyfriends? Billy's so
              intelligent? Cheers.

KATIE   I think you should go home.

PETE   I think so, too. There's chewing gum all
              over the bottom of the table, by the way.
              [He moves to exit. She stops him by speaking]

KATIE   Pete... you're right.

PETE   You put the gum there?

KATIE   No. *[Pause]* The feeling of betrayal is
              worse than if we'd been caught.

PETE   Yeah. I know what you mean.

[They sneak off-stage... Lights fade to blackout.]

17. The perfect family

In which we meet a living, breathing family that is perfect.

Theme
The myth of the 'perfect' family.

Characters
Paul – The father.
Pat – The mother.
Peter – The oldest son.
Penny – The oldest daughter.
Polly – The youngest daughter.

Setting
The Perfect living room.

[Pat enters wearing an apron and carrying a duster. She moves about pleasantly and with a sense of purpose.]

PAT   My, what a beautiful day it's been. How I *love* to vacuum and dust my lovely home. *[A sudden, delightful thought]* Maybe I'll even have time to polish the blades in the waste disposal!

[Peter enters with schoolbooks.]

PETER   Hello, Mother.

PAT   Peter, you're home from school. *[Kisses him lightly]* I thought you had a student government meeting today.

PETER   It went like clockwork. They voted unanimously to start a mandatory school-wide activity to visit the elderly every Friday night.

PAT   They accepted your plan! That's wonderful. Electing you president was the best thing that school could have done. I'm so proud of you.

PETER   *[With all humility, looks down, shuffles feet]* Aw, Mum.

PAT   Where is your sister Penny? You usually carry her books as you walk home from school.

PETER   She's staying late to teach calculus to some of the students who are having problems. She's leading the interpretative dance class, too.

PAT   That Penny's from heaven. She's one of a kind.

PETER   She certainly is. I'm proud to be her brother.

PAT   I had better fix dinner before your father gets home. He wanted to take us out to eat at Antoine's tonight but I had my heart set on cooking.

PETER   Is there anything I can do to help – set the table, pour the milk, take out the rubbish?

PAT   No thank you, darling.

PETER   Then I think I'll go to my room to get the creases out of my bedsheets. *[Moves to exit]*

PAT   Don't you have a date tonight with Melissa?

PETER   Yes, I do. I'll pick her up after our family meal.

PAT   She's such a nice girl.

PETER   I'm so happy you approve, Mother. *[He exits]*

PAT   *[Sighs contentedly]* What a good boy. *[Polly enters looking slightly messy]* Polly, where have you been? I was wondering about you.

POLLY   I decided to weed the garden and trim the bushes around the house.

PAT   What an industrious little lady you are! You must be starving after all that work. I'm going to fix meatloaf and spinach for dinner.

POLLY   Spinach! My favourite! I'll go wash my hands right away so I can help you! *[She rushes off. Again, Pat sighs with deep contentment]*

PAT   What did I do to deserve such blessed children?

[Paul enters – dressed for work and carrying flowers.]

PAUL   Honey, I'm home.

PAT   *[Moving to him for a hug]* Hello, darling.

[He presents the flowers.]

PAUL   For you.

PAT   *[Taking them]* For me? *Again?*

PAUL   Who else?

PAT   But this is the seventh time this week!

PAUL   Really? I must be slacking off. An entire garden
          wouldn't be enough for you.

PAT   You're so poetic. Thank you. They're beautiful.
          [She kisses him lightly] And to reciprocate your
          generosity, I'm going to fix you a scrumptious
          dinner as an indication of my sincere gratitude!

PAUL   Are you *sure* you don't want to go out to eat?

PAT   I'm sure. I *want* to make you dinner. But I *will*
          need to go to the mall later if you don't mind.

PAUL   The credit card is all yours. Get whatever you
          want.

PAT   Not what I want, darling, only what I *need. [She
          exits wistfully]*

PAUL   What a woman!

*[He sits down with a newspaper and begins reading. Penny
enters carrying her schoolbooks. She looks forlorn.]*

PENNY   Hello, Father. *[She kisses him on the cheek]*

PAUL   Hi, Penny. How was your day?

PENNY   It was all right, I suppose. I learned some
          interesting things in chemistry.

[Polly enters.]

POLLY   Hi, Dad. Hi, Penny. I'm glad you're home. May
          I borrow one of your blouses for my drama
          meeting tonight?

PENNY   Of course you may. Anything in my wardrobe is
          yours to wear.

POLLY   Thank you. *[She exits]*

PENNY   I think I'll practise piano for an hour. *[She moves to exit]*

PAUL   *[With perceptive concern]* Penny... is everything all right?

PENNY   *[Pauses]* Why do you ask?

PAUL   *[Chuckles knowingly]* Angel, I'm your father. I can tell when something is troubling you. You normally like to practise your piano for *two* hours.

PENNY   Well...

PAUL   *[Pats the chair next to him]* Come here and tell me all about it. *[She does]* What's wrong?

PENNY   *[Hesitantly]* The girls at school were teasing me.

PAUL   They were? Why?

PENNY   They said that I'm not real. They think I'm strange.

PAUL   That's silly.

PENNY   They say we're airheads because we never have any problems. We're not airheads, are we, Dad?

PAUL   No, of course not.

PENNY   And they say we're weird because we don't have any problems.

PAUL   We have problems, Penny.

PENNY   We do?

PAUL   Of course we do.

PENNY   Oh. *[Pausing to think about it]* For example?

PAUL   For example... well, ah... we... *[Pauses to think]* Remember that time we...? Oh, that worked out fine. Ah... well... *[Suddenly realises]* This whole conversation is a problem!

PENNY   It is?

PAUL   Yes, because I can't think of anything wrong. So there. Just tell your friends that they should learn from our example and try to get along with their families. Should we go out of our way to fight just to please them?

PENNY   No. I don't suppose so.

PAUL   There you are then.

PENNY   Thanks, Dad, that was easy. Why didn't I think of all that? *[She hugs him appreciatively]*

PAUL   You're young. One day you will.

PENNY   Thank you. I feel much better.

[Peter enters, dressed for his date.]

PETER   Hi, Dad. Hello, Penny. You look very nice today.

PENNY   Thank you.

PAUL   Why are you so dressed up, young man?

PETER   I'm going out with Melissa tonight.

PAUL   *[Smiles]* Ah, she's a nice girl.

PETER   *[Sudden idea]* Hey, would all of you like to come along? It'd be brilliant if everyone went with us.

[Polly enters as the conversation continues.]

PENNY   No, thank you. I need to practise my piano... for *two* hours. *[She smiles knowingly at her father. He smiles back with a wink]*

POLLY   Dad, may I please have a ride to drama club after dinner?

PETER   I would love to take you, Polly.

[Pat enters.]

PAT   You're all here. Good. Dinner's ready.

PAUL   *[Standing]* Wonderful! Let me wash my hands and I'll be right there.

PAT   Children? *[She gestures to the kitchen and they move very mannerly]*

PENNY   I can hardly wait. Suddenly I feel very hungry.

POLLY   Yes, I'm famished as well.

PETER   I'm sure it will be delicious.

[Paul and Pat embrace.]

PAUL   Is this a great family or what?

PAT   Yes... we're perfect!

[They exit.]

Blackout. [Curtain.]

18. Let's call the whole thing off

In which two boys and two girls explore the differences in their genders.

Theme
Misunderstanding the differences between boys and girls.

Characters
Neil – a pre-adolescent boy.
Tony – a pre-adolescent boy.
Jenny – a pre-adolescent girl.
Karen – a pre-adolescent girl.

Setting
A school cafeteria, café, or anywhere students might gather to do homework (or socialise).

[A school cafeteria or café. Stage right, two young women, pre-teens, sit down with their books to study. After a moment, stage left, two young men, also pre-teens, enter. One of them – Tony, who is carrying a couple of books – stops for a second when he sees the girls – but sits down. Neil is in the middle of a story, but Tony is trying to casually look at the girls.]

NEIL   So Mr Hildreth says, 'What's the matter with you, Neil? You're throwing like a woman.' So I say, 'No, I don't. *I* throw like *this*.' *[He gives a demonstration of his rather masculine throwing style]* 'And a *woman* throws like *this*.' *[He gives a demonstration of a rather feminine throwing technique]* And Mr Hildreth sent me to the showers for answering back. That wasn't answering back. Do you think it was answering back? Tony? Hey, Tony.

TONY   *[Clearly distracted]* Hmm?

NEIL   I was talking to you.

TONY   Yeah, I know. Mr Hildreth. *[He glances at the girls]*

NEIL   What's the matter with you?

TONY   Nothing.

NEIL   It's something.

TONY   It's nothing. I was just… you know.

NEIL   No, I don't know.

TONY   Then forget about it.

NEIL   Forget about what?

TONY   Nothing. Did we come here to do our homework or what?

NEIL   I came here became Mr Hildreth told me to.

TONY   Well, shut up and do your homework.

[He opens a book and makes as if he's reading it. But his eye wanders over to the girls.]

NEIL   All right. *[Beat, he's empty-handed]* What am I supposed to study?

[Our focus now shifts to the girls. Karen is reading intently. Jenny is aware that Tony is watching them.]

JENNY   I don't believe it. Do you see that?

KAREN   *[Looking up]* See what?

JENNY   Don't look! *[Beat]* Over there.

KAREN   *[Looks off in the wrong direction]* What?

JENNY   Not that way, stupid. The other way. It's Tony and Creepface.

KAREN   Oh. *[She starts to wave and calls out]* Hi, Ton –

JENNY   *[Instantly putting her hand over Karen's mouth]* Are you crazy?

KAREN   *[Through Jenny's hand]* What? *[Pushes hand away]* What's wrong?

JENNY   You can't wave at them.

KAREN   Why not?

JENNY   Because it's just what they want you to do. Tony's been sitting there just waiting for you to wave.

KAREN   So? I like Tony.

JENNY   What?

KAREN   I like Tony.

JENNY   But you can't! He's... he's one of *them.*

KAREN   One of *what?*

JENNY   You know. A *boy*.

KAREN   *[Teasing]* Really? Are you sure?

JENNY   Yeah, I'm sure. And if you wave at him, then he'll come over and talk to you and then – bang – that's it.

KAREN   What's it?

JENNY   He'll be all over you like white on rice.

KAREN   *What?!*

JENNY   My older sister told me all about it.

KAREN   All about what? Rice?

JENNY   No. Boys and how they are.

KAREN   How are they?

JENNY   Awful – if you listen to my sister. She reads a lot. Pay any attention to them and they're like little puppy dogs.

KAREN   They drool and pee on the carpet?

JENNY   Worse. They wanna, like, kiss you and stuff.

KAREN   Stuff? What kind of stuff?

JENNY   Stuff, like sitting in a chair and watching TV and belching at the football matches before they fall asleep.

KAREN   That's what happens after they kiss you?

JENNY   Uh huh.

KAREN   That sounds awful.

JENNY   I told you.

[At this point, Tony has caught Karen's eye and waves. She smiles and waves back.]

JENNY   Stop that!

[Our perspective shifts to the boys.]

TONY   Do you ever think about girls, Neil?

NEIL   What?

TONY   Girls. You know.

NEIL   Why would I think about girls? I've got hobbies.

TONY   Yeah, but...

NEIL   You've been thinking about girls.

TONY   Well, yeah...

NEIL   I knew it! I knew it!

TONY   What?

NEIL   I could tell. It's because you started getting hair under your armpits.

TONY   How do you know about that?

NEIL   Last time I spent the night at your house. You can't fool me. *[Groans]* I knew it was coming. Kiss your life goodbye.

TONY   What're you talking about?

NEIL   I got the whole story from my Dad. He started shaving and then the hormones took over and the next thing he knew, he was married.

TONY   Hormones? Don't they come knocking on your door and try to make you read their magazines?

NEIL   I don't know what you call it. All I know is my Dad said the girls were hanging around him like flies on an outdoor loo. I think it was his aftershave.

TONY   His aftershave smells like an outdoor loo?

NEIL   I don't know. I've never been in an outdoor loo.
Anyway, you have to watch yourself. He told
me it's the worst thing in the world.

TONY   What is?

NEIL   Liking girls. It'll ruin your life.

TONY   I don't get it.

NEIL   Well, for one thing, he said you never know
what they want. Even when they tell you, it
may not *really* be what they want. He said
mind-reading comes in handy if you can figure
out how to do it.

TONY   You and your Dad had a long talk about this,
Hmm?

NEIL   Yeah. It was his 'birds and the bees' speech –
but he never got around to the part about sex.
He just started talking about women and then I
finally walked out.

TONY   Why'd you walk out?

NEIL   He started to cry. I hate it when my old man
cries.

TONY   He cries a lot?

NEIL   Only when he talks about women. One minute
he's saying how great it was when he was
sixteen and going out on a date with a girl in a
sweater named Marilyn – and the next minute
he's crying. This is what they do to you.

TONY   My Dad never tells me anything.

NEIL   I got the whole scoop.

[Our perspective goes back to the girls.]

KAREN   What do you think they're talking about?

JENNY   Probably sports or torturing kittens or something. They're Neanderthals.

KAREN   You don't think Tony's cute?

JENNY   Compared to a squashed bug, maybe. On his own, I wouldn't use a word like 'cute'.

KAREN   What word would you use?

JENNY   'Hopeless'. Definitely 'hopeless'. All boys are hopeless.

KAREN   Why do you say that?

JENNY   Because that's what my Mum says to my Dad all the time. 'Harry, you're hopeless,' she says.

KAREN   Why?

JENNY   I suppose because he's hopeless. Last week was their anniversary and he bought her a waste disposal. That's when she said he was hopeless. He didn't get it. He said she'd been complaining about a waste disposal for three years and when he finally gets her one, she says he's hopeless. He got mad and she got mad and they yelled and finally Mum shoved her present for Dad down the waste disposal.

KAREN   What did she get him?

JENNY   My sister told me later it was some kind of lingerie.

KAREN   Lingerie?

JENNY   Yeah – something like that. I don't speak Italian.

KAREN   But isn't lingerie, like, undies? Why would your

Mum buy your Dad undies for their anniversary?

JENNY   They weren't for *him*. They were for her to wear *around* him. Do I have to explain everything?

KAREN   Yeah.

JENNY   Well I can't. All I know is she shoved them down the waste disposal and one of the clasps got caught and it broke the sink. My Dad worked on it for three hours and let me tell you it wasn't a pretty sight. My Mum says that, like most men, my Dad isn't very good with fixing things, even though he thinks he is.

KAREN   My Dad's like that. He ruined our car.

JENNY   Well, first my Dad wouldn't ring the plumber – which is what my Mum wanted him to do in the first place. He said he didn't want to pay the plumber fifty quid to come fix something he could fix himself. So Mum handed him the home DIY book I got him for Christmas, but he said he didn't need it because plumbing was easy and he bet he could even recover her lingerie for her to wear later. And then when the water started pouring all over the floor, he broke one of the cupboard doors with a wrench.

KAREN   Why did he do that?

JENNY   Because Mum said he was hopeless again. The sink still isn't fixed. I have to wash the dishes in the bathtub.

KAREN   Do you think Tony is like that?

JENNY   If he isn't now, he will be.

[Our perspective goes back to the boys.]

TONY   So let me get this straight. Girls get mad for no reason at all and then get even madder because guys can't figure out why they're mad in the first place?

NEIL   Right. I've seen it with my own two eyes. It has something to do with a... a... I don't know, some kind of punctuation mark that happens to them every month. *[Remembering]* A comma? No, a period or something.

TONY   As in history?

NEIL   I suppose. But you better watch out when it happens. My Dad says that wrestling naked with a pit bull dog is safer than trying to talk to my Mum when she gets like that.

TONY   My Mum gets in funny moods, but I don't think it's ever that bad.

NEIL   Women are sneaky about it. They wait until you least suspect it, then they suddenly scream their heads off because you didn't fold the towel in the bathroom or you left the seat up on the toilet. My Mum nearly put me up for adoption because I left a dirty plate under the recliner.

TONY   I don't think Karen would be like that. She's always smiling.

NEIL   Don't bet on it. Lurking beneath that smile is a Tyrannosaurus rex waiting to turn you into a snack. And they don't do it like blokes do it.

TONY   What do you mean?

NEIL   Well, you know, a bloke will hang out with you if he likes you or he'll punch you if he doesn't, but girls *talk*. My Dad says they're vicious.

Especially when they talk about other girls. Razor sharp. He says they're schemers.

TONY   I don't believe it.

NEIL   Don't kid yourself. They're worse with men. My Dad says my mum is always trying to figure him out, scheming about how to change him.

TONY   Change him?

NEIL   Oh, yeah. He says women are born with a mission to try to make men different from what they are. If a bloke spends his whole life doing something one way, then a girl will spend her whole life trying to make him change it. Look, I'm getting this from someone who knows. My Dad's been fighting change for as long as I can remember.

[Our perspective returns to the girls.]

KAREN   A male *what*?

JENNY   A male ego. I heard my Mum talking about it. That's what makes men act so weird all the time.

KAREN   I don't understand.

JENNY   It's something they're born with. It's a deformity of sorts. Mum says it's what makes them leave the seat up.

KAREN   Oh.

JENNY   And it makes him blow a fuse when Mum wants to go shopping... or when she won't let him kiss her after he's been digging in the garden... or when he spends all day polishing the car but won't clear the rubbish out of the garage... or when he comes home upset because he did an own goal... you get the idea.

KAREN   Sort of.

JENNY   And it's another reason why they don't know how to talk.

KAREN   They don't know how to talk?

JENNY   They sort of grunt when you ask them a question or say 'You know' a lot, as if it's a complete sentence.

KAREN   *[Bewildered]* Then why do men and women ever get together?

JENNY   I have no idea. I think the whole idea is disgusting. I only like my Dad because he isn't a boy anymore. Can we get out of here now?

KAREN   I suppose.

[They begin to gather their things as our perspective goes back to the boys.]

TONY   *[Alarmed]* They're leaving.

NEIL   Good riddance.

TONY   But... I was thinking... I mean... I wanted to talk to her.

NEIL   Talk to her! About what? That's all they ever do is talk. About what colour dresses they like to wear and who wrote a note about someone else or whether to grow their nails long or put their hair up or buy a new handbag or –

[Tony moves towards Karen.]

NEIL   Hey – wait. Where're you going?

[Jenny sees Tony approaching.]

JENNY   Hurry up, Karen. Let's go.

KAREN   *[Turns towards Karen]* Why? What's the – ? *[Sees
          Tony coming]* Oh.

JENNY   Don't talk to him.

NEIL   Don't do it, Tone.

TONY   Karen?

JENNY   Ignore him.

NEIL   She'll give you pimples.

KAREN   *[Approaches Tony – they meet centre stage]* Hi,
          Tony. What're you doing here?

TONY   Oh, you know.

JENNY   See what I mean? He'll be grunting next.

NEIL   She'll have you parting your hair in a different
          place.

KAREN   We were... doing homework.

TONY   Me, too. I was wondering if... uh... you know,
          maybe... walk home. With me, I mean.
          Together.

KAREN   I'd like that.

TONY   Me, too. Let's go.

KAREN   All right. *[To Jenny]* See you later, Jen.

TONY   *[To Neil]* Neil, I'm gonna... uh, you know.

NEIL   It'll only end in tears.

[Tony and Karen begin to exit.]

KAREN   You don't know anything about plumbing, do
          you?

TONY   No. Why?

[They exit. Neil and Jenny are left facing each other.]

JENNY   So what're *you* looking at, creepface?

NEIL   I was just wondering if I'll ever get so desperate
         that I'll wanna walk home with someone like
         you.

JENNY   Don't be sick, you Neanderthal. *[She turns to exit
         in the opposite direction]*

NEIL   Yeah? I hope you, you know, choke on a bug.
         [He turns to exit in the opposite direction]

JENNY   *[Over her shoulder]* In your dreams, worm-lips.

NEIL   *[Over his shoulder]* Any dream with you would
         be a nightmare, barf-breath!

JENNY   *[As she exits]* Oh yeah?

NEIL   *[As he exits]* Yeah!

[They exit in opposite directions.]

Blackout. [Curtain.]

19. The home group

In which we get to see the birth, development, and dissolution of a home Bible study group.

Theme
Personal relationships in a Christian setting.

Characters
Charles – The group leader. Very enthusiastic.
Bob – Dogmatic.
Henry – Equally dogmatic.
Dave – A fairly laid-back (if not scandalous) accountant.
Lana – A very withdrawn woman.
Beatrice – A modern woman.
Elaine – An average girl.
Narrator.

Setting
Charles's living room.

[A small circle of chairs. Several people – Charles, Bob, Henry, Dave, Lana, Beatrice and Elaine – along with a few extras, enter and sit down. The Bible study leader, Charles, has a guitar in hand. They 'freeze' in a seated position until the Narrator has spoken.]

NARRATOR   One of the great ministries of the church is the local Home Bible Study Group. It can be an opportunity for people of diverse backgrounds to come together in unity, study their Bibles, and share in mutual fellowship and development as believers. It can be the one night of the week that serves to energise and motivate. It can be a place to open hearts up – to be vulnerable, to question, to doubt, to reaffirm. It can be all these things.

It *can* be.

Let's drop in on Charles, our novice Group Leader, and one particular Bible Study Group as it meets for the first time.

Any resemblance between the Bible Study you are about to see and those currently in existence is a shame.

[With that said, he turns and exits. Charles immediately begins strumming away at the guitar – almost frantically – with barely distinguishable chords. He sings a popular chorus song – with equal energy. Everyone else sits and looks at him blankly.]

CHARLES   Okay! One more time on that chorus!

[He sings a portion of the song again – still no one joining in – the same blank looks – he comes to a big finish and, obviously out of breath, laughs and puts the guitar aside.]

CHARLES   Don't you love those praise choruses?

[Blank looks.]

CHARLES   Yeah, well, they certainly minister to me. Welcome to our very first Home Group. I'm delighted you're all here. I am, of course, anticipating an incredible time to study our Bibles and cultivate personal growth in Christ and to discover the kinds of sharing that'll build friendships and support each other through prayer and encouragement.

BOB   *[Spoken sternly, challenging]* Do you believe in a pre-trib, mid-trib, or post-trib rapture?

CHARLES   Hmm?

BOB   Pre-, mid-, or post-trib rapture?

CHARLES   Well... ah... I'll take it any way I can get it. *[Laughs]* Only joking. I think there's a different Bible study group dealing with those questions. This is the study of the Book of Leviticus – and an exciting book it is, too – with lots of laws to draw practical application from. Now the way I see it: we should sing first, like we just did, then maybe enjoy a time for prayer requests and personal intimate encounters, then the Bible Study and Lana – raise your hand, Lana, just in case we don't have all the names down yet –

[Blank looks, Lana – the wallflower – hangs her head shyly and raises her hand ever so slightly.]

CHARLES   Lana is providing the food and refreshments tonight. What did you bring, Lana?

LANA   *[Almost inaudibly]* Mars Bars and Lucozade.

CHARLES   Oh, don't be so shy, Lana. We're one big open family here – right, gang?

[Blank looks.]

CHARLES	Of course we are. Now, what did you say you brought, Lana?

LANA	*[Louder but still soft]* Mars Bars and Lucozade.

CHARLES	Mars Bars and Lucozade. *[Tries to subdue his nausea]* Yeah, right, and we'll be looking forward to that a little later in the evening. What do you say we take prayer requests and enjoy some personal share-time?

[Blank looks.]

BOB	Do you believe in immediate, mediate or the Augustine viewpoint on the imputation of sin?

CHARLES	Hmm?

BOB	Do you believe – ?

CHARLES	Why don't we save questions for the Bible study portion of the evening? Does anybody have anything they want to share personally at this time?

[Blank looks.]

CHARLES	What has the Lord done in your life? Anything?

[Blank looks.]

CHARLES	Has he taught you anything recently?

[Blank looks.]

CHARLES	Are there any prayer requests?

[Blank looks.]

CHARLES	Does anybody know what time it is?

[Blank looks.]

BOB   *[Looking at watch]* It is 8:05.

CHARLES   Great. Henry, why don't you dismiss us with prayer?

[They freeze in place as the Narrator enters again.]

NARRATOR   It's true. The first meeting is often a little... uncomfortable. But let's look at the same Bible study about a month later. Notice the intensity, the zeal to discuss...

[The group 'unfreezes' in the midst of an argument as the Narrator exits.]

BOB   But the theological ramifications are staggering if what you say is true! The whole foundations of Christianity would shift!

HENRY   You're making a big deal out of nothing! I truly believe that God – in his love and mercy – wouldn't penalise the innocent like that! It would suggest that he is not who he claims he is!

BOB   No, no, no! It *reinforces* who he says he is!

CHARLES   *[Trying to get control]* Pardon me...

HENRY   Show me Scripture on that!

CHARLES   All right, everyone! Hold on.

BOB   Show me Scripture supporting *your* conclusions –

CHARLES   Whoa! We've gone a little off the track here. Now, I think we should simply go ahead and *pray* for Lana's budgie and let God do as he will. No harm in trying. But I'm *not* sure that the bird's illness is indicative of sin in Lana's life. Right, Lana?

LANA   Oh, I *hope* not. Well, I don't think so. Of
            course not. Oh, that poor bird.

CHARLES   Okay. Right. *[Trying to be encouraging]* But,
            hey, I appreciate everyone getting involved
            like that. It's good to have somebody talking
            other than me.

BOB   Amen.

CHARLES   But, I'll tell you what – let's save the
            theological debate for *after* prayer time.
            Okay? Now, are there any other prayer
            requests?

[Blank looks.]

CHARLES   Would someone like to lead us, then?

[Blank looks.]

CHARLES   Aw, come on, guys. Surely *somebody* wants to
            pray.

[Lana sheepishly raises her hand.]

CHARLES   *[Encouraged]* There you go. Good for you,
            Lana.

LANA   I don't want to pray. I was just wondering if
            I could retract the prayer request for my
            budgie? It really *might* be sin in my life.

CHARLES   But... it's our only prayer request. We won't
            have anything to pray for it you retract it.

LANA   Well... go ahead, then. If anything happens,
            I'll just buy another one. They're not hard to
            get.

CHARLES   Thanks. I guess *I'll* lead.

[Bowing their heads, they freeze as the Narrator enters.]

NARRATOR   The same Bible study. The eighth week. As

time has moved on, our group has become unified in spirit and emotion – reaching the pinnacle of everything this group could hope to be. Everyone begins to share willingly during the course of the evening – sometimes leaving the members drained emotionally when things wind down.

[Narrator exits. The group 'unfreezes' and looks somewhat drained emotionally. There is a tell-tale quiet about them. Everyone is smiling pleasantly – looking one to another. One or two reach over and place their hands on the shoulder or hand of the person next to them – or other gestures of affection.]

CHARLES   What a night it's been, Hmm? I never would have expected the Levitical laws on leprosy to bring out so much in us.

[There are a few chuckles.]

CHARLES   I don't know about you but I'm drained. Lana, thank you for sharing that experience with us. I think we all now have a greater understanding of what it's like to be married six times.

LANA   Seven.

CHARLES   Seven. That's right. What pain, what suffering!

LANA   *I've* suffered, too.

CHARLES   I'm sure you have. Wow. You know, when we started this group, I thought I'd need a crowbar to get a word out of you. *Any* of you. But, when you open up, you *really* open up. And Beatrice thanks for showing us the snapshots of your trip to the Cotswolds.

BEATRICE   The Lake District.

CHARLES   Right. Those shots of your cousins breeding cattle were... well, I can't even think of the word. *[Dave gestures that he wants to speak]* Go ahead, Dave.

DAVE   I don't know about you guys but... I feel like something special has happened between us tonight. I feel closer to you guys now than I have to anyone in my whole life. I know I confessed some things tonight that I've never told anyone before. And because of that, I feel like God has forgiven me for the wrongs I've done and maybe... maybe I can forgive myself, too. Maybe I can even give back the half-a-million I embezzled from my company.

[Everyone nods affirmatively.]

CHARLES   I'm sure you can, Dave. *[To Bob]* And you'll be taking over as treasurer next week, right, Bob? *[To Dave]* Nothing personal, of course.

DAVE   That's all right.

CHARLES   And I'm glad you're here, Dave. I thank God for you. For *all* of you. *[Pause]* Well... I suppose we should say goodnight. What time is it, anyway?

HENRY   Almost midnight.

CHARLES   *[Chuckles]* We ran a little overtime.

BEATRICE   Only two-and-a-half hours.

CHARLES   Should we have a whip-round for your baby-sitter?

BEATRICE   *[Amused]* It might help.

DAVE   I'll pass the hat around in a minute.

CHARLES   Ah, Bob... why don't you take over as
treasurer *this* week? *[After a thoughtful pause]*
... I'd like to say that this is the kind of night
that makes me glad I'm doing this Bible
study. Even the pistachio and raisin pie was
exceptionally interesting, Lana. *[Pauses]* Let's
close with a word of prayer...

*[They bow their heads and 'freeze' in place as the Narrator
enters.]*

NARRATOR   The twelfth week. Our Bible study has gone
one step beyond their unity of purpose to
complete comfort with each other... and a
thoroughly casual attitude about why they're
meeting.

*[As the Narrator exits, the group comes up from prayer.
Everyone gets comfortable, relaxed.]*

CHARLES   Amen. Okay, let's open up to Leviticus...

[Movement is slow, very casual.]

HENRY   *[To Dave]* I have passes to the Manchester
United game Friday night. Are you
interested? *[Even as he speaks, Lana leans to
Beatrice and begins a separate conversation]*

DAVE   Friday? I don't think I have anything
planned. Let me give you a ring tomorrow.

LANA   My sister-in-law has a pair of shoes just like
yours.

BEATRICE   She does?

LANA   I think hers may be a little lighter colour,
though.

BEATRICE   I saw those. I got these because they match a
dress I bought at Marks and Sparks.

CHARLES   Leviticus, people.

ELAINE   *[Joining in the conversation with Beatrice and Lana]* Do you like the lower heels or the higher ones?

BEATRICE   I like the lower heels.

BOB   *[To Henry]* I was reading last week that the work on the motorway has been postponed *again*. It takes me almost an hour to get to the office now.

LANA   My husband likes the higher heels.

BEATRICE   Your husband wears high heels?

[They laugh.]

LANA   Not with *his* legs.

CHARLES   Hello?

[They laugh again.]

HENRY   I'm not surprised. I've been trying to go in to work earlier but the traffic seems just as bad.

ELAINE   I need lower heels for work. I don't think I could make it a full day with the high heels.

DAVE   My office is considering a rotation schedule.

BEATRICE   *[Proudly]* I got promoted the day before yesterday.

BOB   A lot of offices are going to that.

LANA   You did? That's terrific!

DAVE   I wouldn't mind it. I get tired

sitting in the rush-
hour.

HENRY   I read the paper.

*[Charles picks up the guitar and destroys another praise
chorus with his playing and singing. They stop, look at him.]*

CHARLES   *[Puts guitar down]* I thought that would get
your attention. *[Gestures to Bible]* Leviticus?
Third book of the Bible? Please?

BOB   *[Slowly getting his Bible]* Did you know that
the Hebrew Bible has a different number of
books in it than ours? They combine I and II
Kings, Chronicles, Samuel...

DAVE   I suppose sequels weren't as important to
them as they are to us.

HENRY   I heard a rumour that Sylvester Stallone is
going to do another *Rocky* film.

BOB   Who could be left for him to fight?

DAVE   Terminator 14.

BEATRICE   Did you like the *Terminator* films?

ELAINE   Oh yes.

BEATRICE   I thought they were amazing.

ELAINE   Who didn't?

*[Charles turns sideways on his chair and rests his head in his
hand resignedly.]*

CHARLES   Familiarity breeds distraction.

BOB   I thought it was 'contempt'.

CHARLES   That's next.

[They 'freeze'. The Narrator enters again. As he does, everyone except Charles and Bob exits.]

NARRATOR   And, finally... the last week of the Bible study.

[Narrator exits. Charles and Bob 'unfreeze' and look at each other.]

CHARLES   Well, what do you think? Should we start or wait a few minutes longer?

BOB   It's almost 8:30. We should start. I don't think anyone else is coming.

CHARLES   I wonder what happened to everyone? This is our last class. You would have thought they'd make it for this.

BOB   I know Henry said something about being out of town. Beatrice is in some tennis tournament. And I suppose you read in the paper about Dave.

CHARLES   Yeah... *[Confounded]* You know, he told me he gave the money back.

BOB   I'm sure it was all a misunderstanding. His wife'll have him bailed out tonight.

CHARLES   Good. Okay, let's start. *[He reaches to pick up the guitar]*

BOB   Ah, Charles... you don't have to do that.

CHARLES   No songs?

BOB   No songs. To be quite honest, we've never liked the songs. We've been trying to figure out how to tell you short of giving you money for guitar lessons.

CHARLES   Oh.

BOB   Obviously we're not the musical types.

CHARLES   I suppose not. *[Looks to the empty room]* So this is how it ends. My first outing as group leader. We were supposed to do evaluations tonight.

BOB   Do you want me to do one?

CHARLES   Not really.

BOB   I would if you wanted. I think you've done a smashing job. This group has meant a lot to me even with its oddities. *[Pause]* I'm going to miss Lana's surprise snacks.

CHARLES   Me, too. The chocolate chip watermelon was my favourite.

[Long pause.]

CHARLES   I haven't had dinner. Do you want to go out for some pizza?

BOB   Yeah.

[They stand, begin to exit.]

BOB   By the way... What *do* you believe in? A pre-trib, mid-trib, or post-trib rapture?

CHARLES   I don't know. What's a trib?

[They exit. Narrator enters again.]

NARRATOR   And that was the beginning of a beautiful friendship.

[Narrator exits.]

Blackout. [Curtain.]

20. The big match

In which two young men try to articulate their deepest thoughts and struggles – during a football match.

Theme
The meaning of masculinity in friendship, communication, failure and a time of crisis.

Characters
John – the football enthusiast.
Ben – the friend with a problem.

Setting
John's home. The room with the telly.

Note
This sketch is about how inarticulate we often are, using gestures and grunts in place of words, to convey our meaning. I've put the 'missing words' in brackets, but you'll have to figure out the corresponding sound or gesture to make the word clear.

[John enters. He is juggling a bowl of crisps, pretzels and more cans of drinks than one person can handle. It's a World Cup kind of occasion and John is geared up. He looks around and realises he doesn't have enough chairs (in fact, there aren't any). He growls and, still balancing the food and drinks, goes off stage only to return a moment later with the food, the drinks and a couple of folding chairs. What follows is an amazing feat of balance as John tries to unfold the chairs and set them up without putting down the food and drinks. At its most comical, Ben – still dressed in a suit from work – arrives and rescues him.]

BEN   What on earth are you – ?

JOHN   You're late.

[Ben helps John get set up as they talk, though Ben's enthusiasm isn't as great as John's.]

BEN   Work. Y'know.

JOHN   The match starts in – what? Two minutes? *[Turns on TV]*

BEN   Hey – *[Spreads his arms as if to say 'I know and I'm sorry I'm late but I got stuck at the office']* All right?

JOHN   Big match. Really big match.

BEN   *[Pulls at his tie, takes off coat]* I'm here.

JOHN   *[Nods and gestures to TV as if to say 'I've been waiting all day for this']* Man!

BEN   Yeah. Your mother?

JOHN   No way. Out. I said, 'Big match. You take the rug-rats and – gone.' Can't have a lot of y'know when I'm trying to watch. *[Gestures to TV, moves feet as if kicking a ball]*

BEN   I didn't even go home first. My Dad and Mum

would've had me going *[Doing things around the house]* and y'know not watching and –

JOHN   They don't get it. I try to say, 'Hey, here's why it's so *you know*' and she just – *[Shakes his head as if to say 'She doesn't understand']* Have a pretzel. *[Suddenly shouts at TV]* Let's go! Do it!

BEN   *[Takes a pretzel, but there's something bothering him]* Yeah!

JOHN   I need this. I don't want to get all, you know, philosophy and stuff, but there are times. There are really times.

BEN   I know.

JOHN   It's like you want to get right down there on the field and – man. Win. Have to win.

BEN   I know.

JOHN   That's what it's all about. The game, right? It's life. Forget all that y'know – fair play – sportsmanship – you have to do what it takes. You have to, y'know, be good. You have to win.

BEN   *[Thoughtfully]* Win.

JOHN   *[Looks at Ben]* What?

BEN   *[Raises his drink as if in a toast]* Win.

JOHN   *[Responding in kind]* Win! That's right. Success, you know?

BEN   Yeah, success.

JOHN   My old man knew. He drilled it – *[Gestures to his brain]* – day in, day out.

BEN   Mine too.

JOHN   The only way. He could have been a great player. Or a coach. Man, he was never the same after he died. *[Suddenly shouts at TV]* Get him! Get him! *[Disappointed]* Awwww.

BEN *[Ponders his drink]* My Dad. I have to make it, he said. I have to make it. I should ring y'know – Mum.

JOHN She knows.

BEN Knows what?

JOHN You're here.

BEN Yeah. I think. Maybe – no, I said so. *[Stands, tugs at tie]* I should've gone y'know *[home]* first. Got out of this suit. *[Pause]* It was no good.

JOHN *[Shouts at TV]* Are you blind? What're you – ? Wait. Yes. Yes. Yes! Do it! Do it! *[To Ben, gestures to TV]* You see? That's what I'm talking about. You know where you are in the game. The rules – you know.

BEN I know.

JOHN And you sweat and work and, there it is, you get to be the best. That's what it's all about.

BEN Yeah, sure. But how're you supposed to – you know?

JOHN What?

BEN It's just – *[Gestures as if to say 'I'm really confused about this']* What if – you know?

JOHN What?

BEN Nothing.

JOHN What?

BEN Nothing.

JOHN What?

BEN   I mean, it's not always – you know – like that.

JOHN   What're you – ?

BEN   They called me in. Sat me down.

JOHN   Work?

BEN   Sacked.

JOHN   When?

BEN   Today. This afternoon.

JOHN   No way.

BEN   I blew it.

JOHN   Not a chance.

BEN   I was bad at it. Always was.

JOHN   Oh man.

BEN   Kept waiting for them to, you know, figure it out. I wasn't fooling anybody.

JOHN   You fooled me.

BEN   I had to work twice as hard as y'know, everybody else just to keep up. You don't know. Man, the stress.

JOHN   I don't believe it. How can – I mean – no way.

BEN   What am I gonna do?

JOHN   Your parents.

BEN   That's why I didn't go home first. How am I supposed to tell them?

JOHN   I don't know. I don't believe it.

BEN   What am I gonna do?

JOHN   I don't know.

BEN   You have to help me, John. I feel like – I'm a –

JOHN   I'm, you know, I'm – *[He spreads arms as if to say, 'I'm here for you, Ben]* I'm here. *[Beat]* These crisps need a dip.

BEN   *[Moves to exit]* Dip. Right. You, uh – *[want something]*?

JOHN   No.

BEN   Watch the match. It'll all… you know. *[Exits]*

JOHN   Yeah. I know. I'll get it sorted. *[Beat]* That's all I have to do. A, you know, game plan. That's what my Dad always said. You have to have a game plan. You have to take action. It's not like it's gonna – I mean, it doesn't just fall into place. You have to make it happen. A game plan. Then you can score. Can't sit around waiting like a bunch of women at a Sunday afternoon tea. No. Get a grip on it and *[growls as if charging]*. Have to be tough. Y'know, work hard. Be strong. Take Action! Make it happen. Be successful. *[Pause, sits down]* But what if the game plan just goes *[makes a breaking-wind noise]*? What if Dad has it all wrong?

Blackout. [Curtain.]

21. Stations of the cross:
a news report

In which a television news team covers Jesus' dramatic journey through the 'Stations of the Cross'.

Theme
The crucifixion of Jesus.

Characters
News Anchor, Ted Goodnuff.
Lynn Wrestle.
Peter.
Woman.
Bill Turnoff.
Jane Paltry.
Malchus.
Gary Litmus.
Professor Ezekiel Rabinowitz.
Pilate.
Deborah.
Barbara Bovril.
Claudius.
Stewart Venison.

Setting
First-century Jerusalem.

Note

Based on the traditional 'Stations of the Cross', this is a supposed news report chronicling the events leading up to Jesus' crucifixion.

[Our cast are seated with their backs to the audience. Ted Goodnuff, our news anchor, stands at a podium stage left. His manner is typical of any professional news anchor.]

NEWS ANCHOR   This is a BB-Sky Special Report. I'm Ted Goodnuff. Events have unfolded at a staggering pace in downtown Jerusalem, where popular speaker Jesus of Nazareth has been arrested by Temple Guards and tried before a hastily assembled Court of the Sanhedrin. Details are unclear as to the exact charges brought against him, but Lynn Wrestle is live on the scene. Lynn, are you there?

[Quickly, the cast begin to 'mill around' like an expectant crowd. Lynn Wrestle steps forward, microphone in hand, finger to her ear so she can hear her earphone.]

LYNN WRESTLE   I am, Ted – just outside the Temple where an expectant crowd waits to hear news of Jesus of Nazareth. As you know, this former carpenter has been a very controversial personality over the past three years, making friends and enemies alike with his unique brand of speaking. I'll see if I can get reactions from the crowd. *[To a man – Peter, as it turns out]* Excuse me, sir.

PETER   *[Nervously]* What? What do you want?

LYNN WRESTLE   Jesus of Nazareth – do you know him?

PETER	No! What makes you say that? Who said I know him?
LYNN WRESTLE	No one. But you're here and I can only assume you have some interest in what's happening inside.
PETER	No. I'm just here to keep warm by the fire. I don't know the man.

[A woman in the crowd steps forward.]

WOMAN	Wait a minute. What are you talking about? You're one of his disciples. I saw you with him. You used to be a farmer – no, a fisherman. Peter. That's it. What do you mean you don't know him?
PETER	I said I don't know him and I don't! Leave me alone!

[He rushes through the crowd as a cock crows in the distance.]

WOMAN	I tell you, he's lying.
LYNN WRESTLE	What's your part in all this?
WOMAN	Who me? Oh, I happened to be out walking the dog, saw the crowd, thought I'd see what was happening. I didn't expect any of *this*.
LYNN WRESTLE	Any of what?
WOMAN	Arresting that Jesus. Though I shouldn't be surprised – talking like he did against the religious leaders, driving the moneychangers out of the Temple the other day.
NEWS ANCHOR	Excuse me, Lynn –
LYNN WRESTLE	Yes, Ted?

NEWS ANCHOR   We have Bill Turnoff standing by *inside* the Temple. Bill?

[Lynn and the crowd turn quickly and quietly and sit down as Bill Turnoff steps forward. He speaks as if he is inside a very quiet place.]

BILL TURNOFF   Ted, I'm inside the Temple and have just received word from an informed source that Jesus was arrested for blasphemy and found *guilty* by the Jewish Religious Court – known as the Sanhedrin – but only after Jesus himself admitted to being the Son of God.

NEWS ANCHOR   Is he there, Bill? Can you speak to him?

BILL TURNOFF   I can't, Ted. The Court has ordered that he be condemned to death. But, since they don't have the authority to carry out the sentence, Jesus has been taken to Pontius Pilate.

NEWS ANCHOR   The governor from Rome. Is he expected to agree to their wishes?

BILL TURNOFF   Pilate has been an unpredictable governor so far. It's hard to tell what he'll do.

NEWS ANCHOR   This whole thing has happened so suddenly. Has anyone talked to you about the plan to arrest Jesus? Is this something that's been brewing for a while?

BILL TURNOFF   My impression is that the religious leaders have been waiting for a long time to arrest Jesus, Ted.

NEWS ANCHOR   But why now?

BILL TURNOFF   The Passover, Ted. My informed source
                      tells me the religious leaders feared that
                      Jesus might try to gain new popularity
                      and more followers from the many
                      people who have gathered here for this
                      most important of Jewish feasts. They
                      wanted to grab Jesus before he could
                      cause any trouble.

NEWS ANCHOR   You say he was arrested in a garden at
                      Gethsemane?

BILL TURNOFF   Yes.

NEWS ANCHOR   Well, we have Jane Paltry in
                      Gethsemane. Jane?

*[Bill turns away as Jane steps forward, along with a young
man holding a rag to his ear.]*

JANE   Ted, I'm in a garden in Gethsemane
                      where this young man here claims to
                      have seen the arrest take place. Tell me
                      your name.

MALCHUS   He cut off my ear.

JANE   We'll get to that in a moment. Your
                      name.

MALCHUS   Malchus. But he cut off my ear.

JANE   Yes. But what can you tell me about what
                      happened here tonight?

MALCHUS   It was awful. Really awful. Jesus was here
                      with his disciples and the Temple Guards
                      came in and got him.

JANE   Why were *you* here?

MALCHUS   Me? I'm a servant. I was just tagging
                      along. He cut off my ear.

JANE   You keep saying that. Who did? Jesus?

MALCHUS   No. One of the guys with him. Took out
                a sword and *slash*, lopped it right off.
                [Takes hand away from ear] Look!

JANE   But your ear looks perfectly fine to me.

MALCHUS   That's because he fixed it.

JANE   Who did – the disciple?

MALCHUS   No, Jesus. He just picked up my ear and
                put it back on. It works better than new.
                Go ahead, talk in it.

JANE   You're telling me that someone cut off
                your ear and Jesus magically put it back
                on?

MALCHUS   Nothing magical about it. It was a
                miracle, I reckon. Go ahead, talk in it.

JANE   *[Ignoring him]* Back to you, Ted.

[Jane and Malchus turn away as Ted speaks.]

NEWS ANCHOR   Thank you, Jane. I understand that Gary
                Litmus, our palace correspondent, is
                ready to talk to us. Gary –

*[Gary Litmus steps forward along with the Professor, and our
cast begins making low crowd noises. Two 'guards' from the
cast take an authoritative stance stage right.]*

GARY LITMUS   Ted, I've never seen anything like it. The
                Temple Priests brought Jesus to Pontius
                Pilate who, after a quick interrogation,
                declared him innocent. But the Temple
                Priests persisted in their accusations until
                Pilate decided to leave it to the people. I
                have with me Professor Ezekiel
                Rabinowitz, expert on Temple affairs.

| EZEKIEL | Gary, it's no surprise to me that things have happened this way. Jesus was unconventional, confrontational, and certainly too outspoken for the leadership. Of course they want him dead. What else can you do with someone who claims to be God's only Son? |

| GARY LITMUS | This move of Pilate's to leave the fate of Jesus to the people – what's behind it? |

| EZEKIEL | As a gesture of kindness, he says he's willing to let a prisoner go free in honour of the Passover. I think Pilate expects the people to let Jesus off. It's either Jesus or a murdering thief named Barabbas. |

| GARY LITMUS | Sounds like the choice should be obvious. |

[The crowd begins to say 'Give us Barabbas! Give us Barabbas!' softly, then with increasing volume.]

| PILATE | *[From behind the crowd]* Then what do you want me to do with Jesus? |

[The crowd cries out: 'Crucify him! Crucify him!']

| PILATE | All right! Have it your way! I wash my hands of the whole business![1] |

['Crucify him!' becomes a soft chant. Pilate, wiping his hands with a towel, pushes through the two 'guards' and moves towards Gary Litmus. Gary Litmus tries to get an interview.]

| GARY LITMUS | Governor? Governor! |

| PILATE | They're an unreasonable people! I give them a perfectly obvious choice and what do they do? They're killing the wrong man. |

---

1. The First Station.

GARY LITMUS   Why didn't you assert your authority
                 and let Jesus go yourself?

PILATE   Are you kidding? And have the Temple
                 Priests go blabbing to Caesar that I'm not
                 a strong leader? Not a chance. They want
                 to kill one of their own, then let them.

GARY LITMUS   But –

PILATE   No more questions. I have work to do.

*[Pilate circles back to join the crowd. The guards turn around.
The cast parade in two lines through the audience –
stretching like a 'wall' to keep us from clearly seeing what's
happening between them. They now chant: 'The cross. The
cross.' Again and again.]*

GARY LITMUS   *[Continuing as they go]* It looks as if Jesus
                 will indeed be crucified, Ted. I'm Gary
                 Litmus – for BB-Sky News – the
                 Governor's Palace.

*[He joins the crowd while another correspondent moves up to
the stage. The cast begins a slow trek from the back to the
stage – still in two lines, with a cross between them, lifted
sideways to give the impression that it's being carried by
Jesus, though we don't see him clearly.]*

BARBARA BOVRIL   I'm Barbara Bovril in Jerusalem. It's a
                 gruesome scene from where I stand. A
                 young carpenter from Galilee takes up
                 and carries a heavy wooden cross[2] to its
                 final destination: a place called Golgotha.
                 It's a long walk from the governor's
                 palace to this desolate hill of death. And
                 Jesus, now beaten and bruised, struggles
                 against the pain to –

---

2. The Second Station.

[She is interrupted as the cross suddenly falls behind the cast. There is a commotion.]

BARBARA BOVRIL   Wait. He's fallen![3] But from here it looks as if... as if... he's talking to someone. A woman. I can't see very clearly... something's going on... the Roman soldiers are doing something... I can't see... It's too difficult to see...

[The cast/crowd moves forward slowly for a few steps, but the cross falls again. There is a small commotion, a mix-up, as Barbara continues to speak.]

BARBARA BOVRIL   He's fallen again! Who can estimate the weight of that cross? He carries it as if he has the entire world on his back. It doesn't look as if he can go any further. But... from here it looks as if he's speaking...

[Gary Litmus and a woman (witness) step out and speak as the cast/crowd take the cross to the stage and deposit it there. While they do, they softly chant: 'Lord have mercy' again and again. On the stage, the cross is moved around flat on the floor until the top points to the audience.]

GARY LITMUS   Gary Litmus, on the street for BB-Sky News, with Deborah – a close witness to the commotion we just saw. Deborah, what happened?

DEBORAH   It's terrible. He fell.

GARY LITMUS   We saw that.

DEBORAH   Then he got up and talked to a woman.[4] She was weeping. I'm not easily moved to tears, but when I saw her face...

---

3. The Third Station.
4. The Fourth Station.

GARY LITMUS   Do you know who she was?

DEBORAH   I heard someone say it was his mother.
Imagine it! His mother is here, watching
him die. I don't know how she could
stand it. If it was *my* son carrying that
cross... it'd be like someone taking a
sword and driving it through my heart.
Bitter pain. Bitter, bitter pain.

GARY LITMUS   Did he lift the cross again?

DEBORAH   The poor man. How much do they
expect him to take? He collapsed. Can
you blame him?

GARY LITMUS   What happened?

DEBORAH   The soldiers pulled a man from the
crowd to help him. A foreigner.[5] They
made him help carry the cross. I don't
know why I'm here. This is a terrible
thing to watch. I mean, I've heard this
Jesus talk. He was a good man. Why do
they have to do this to him? I couldn't
help myself. I reached out to wipe his
face.[6] I looked into his face...

GARY LITMUS   Did he speak to you?

DEBORAH   Not to me, no. But he *did* speak. Oh
yes... I'll never forget what he said, right
after he fell again.[7]

GARY LITMUS   What did he say?

DEBORAH   He said, 'Daughters of Jerusalem, do not

---

5. The Fifth Station.
6. The Sixth Station.
7. The Seventh Station.

weep for me, but weep for yourselves and for your children.'[8] And then he fell once more.[9]

NEWS ANCHOR   Gary?

GARY LITMUS   Yes, Ted?

NEWS ANCHOR   We've re-established our link with Barbara Bovril on the scene at Golgotha...

[Gary and Deborah rejoin the cast. Barbara emerges. We hear the distinct sound of nails being hammered into wood.]

BARBARA BOVRIL   Yes, I can hear you, Ted, but we're having technical difficulties. I'm on Golgotha, sadly known as the Skull. As is customary with crucifixions, they have stripped Jesus.[10] That horrible sound you hear is the sound of the nails being driven into his hands and feet.[11] With me now is Claudius Extremitor, former head of the Roman Crucifixion squad.

[Claudius Extremitor approaches her.]

CLAUDIUS   Good afternoon.

BARBARA BOVRIL   Exactly what's going on here?

CLAUDIUS   It's all pretty straightforward, really. We take criminals like this Jesus fellow and we nail their hands and feet to the cross. Then we lift them up – like so –

[The cross is lifted – with its back to us so we can only make out the figure on the cross. The cast/crowd react. Some weeping, some mocking.]

---

8. The Eighth Station.
9. The Ninth Station.
10. The Tenth Station.
11. The Eleventh Station.

CLAUDIUS   And they either die of intense pain, by
                  bleeding to death, or suffocating.

BARBARA BOVRIL   It's horrible.

CLAUDIUS   Yeah. But it's supposed to be. It's a
                  punishment for whatever he's done
                  wrong.

BARBARA BOVRIL   Do you know what Jesus has done
                  wrong?

CLAUDIUS   No. But that's none of my business, is it?

BARBARA BOVRIL   Thank you, Mr Claudius. Ted, I'm going
                  to try to talk to some of the many people
                  who have gathered to –

[She suddenly turns away.]

NEWS ANCHOR   I'm sorry. We seem to have lost contact
                  with Barbara Bovril at Golgotha. Perhaps
                  it would be helpful if we recapped the
                  circumstances leading up to the arrest,
                  trial and crucifixion of this man from
                  Nazareth. He is shrouded in mystery, but
                  – *[beat]* Wait. I understand that Jerusalem
                  has been rocked with violent
                  thunderstorms and… yes, earthquakes.
                  [To someone off] Do we have contact?
                  No… Things are calming down. Can we
                  get to someone in Jerusalem to – *[beat]*
                  Yes. We have local reporter Stewart
                  Venison. Stewart? Can you hear me?

[Stewart steps out from the cast/crowd.]

STEWART   I can, Ted. It's been quite an afternoon
                  here in Jerusalem. Many say they've seen
                  nothing like it. The sky suddenly went
                  dark and the ground shook violently for
                  several minutes. There is a rumour that

it's somehow connected with the death
of Jesus of Nazareth.[12]

NEWS ANCHOR He *has* died, then?

STEWART Yes, Ted. Jesus died around three o'clock
this afternoon. Sources on the scene tell
me that he said several things prior to
his death – but at the very end, he cried
out in a loud voice and said, 'Father, into
your hands I commend my spirit.'

NEWS ANCHOR Can we assume that his body has been
removed from the cross?

STEWART Yes, it has. They took his body down
and, after a time held by Jesus' mother,[13]
he was removed to an unknown tomb.[14]

NEWS ANCHOR What a day his mother has had. Have
you been able to talk to her?

STEWART No. She has been kept in seclusion by
her family and friends. In fact, most of
the people – followers and friends – of
Jesus are not to be found. We don't know
if they've run off out of fear for their
lives, or simply wish to be left alone,
perhaps to get on with their lives *without*
the charismatic leader who caused such a
stir over the last three years.

NEWS ANCHOR Do you think we've heard the last about
Jesus, Stewart?

STEWART There's a story going around that the
Temple Priests have asked the governor

---

12. The Twelfth Station.
13. The Thirteenth Station.
14. The Fourteenth Station.

to post guards by Jesus' tomb. It's been understood by those who heard Jesus preach that he will rise from the dead.

NEWS ANCHOR   Does anyone really believe it?

STEWART   I don't know, Ted. For many, that belief may be the only flicker of light at the end of a very, very dark day. This is Stewart Venison, BB-Sky News, Jerusalem.

[He turns away.]

NEWS ANCHOR   Thank you, Stewart. We will, of course, keep you informed of any further developments in the Middle East. I'm Ted Goodnuff and this has been a special report. We now return you to our regularly scheduled programme. From all of us at BB-Sky, thank you for watching.

Blackout. [Curtain.]

22. The answering machine

In which a relationship ends with terrible consequences.

Theme
The consequences of confusing love with other things.

Characters
Derek.
Mark.
Beth.

Setting
Mark's home. A living room, or place where the
answering machine may be kept.

Scene 1.

[We hear a phone ring, then an answering machine picks up.]

MARK   Hey, you've reached Mark's answering machine
       – which means I'm not around or in the shower
       or ignoring your call. You know the routine:
       leave a message after the tone so I can decide
       whether or not to ring you back. *[Laughs, the
       tone cuts him off]*

BETH   Mark, are you there? Pick up the phone. Come
       on, we need to talk. Mark! *[Sighs]* Okay, fine.
       Ring me.

Scene 2.

*[Rather than the entire message on Mark's machine, we hear
just the tone, then:]*

BETH   Mark... pick up the phone if you're there.
       Seriously. I'm really... *[Beat]* Look, we need to
       talk about last night. We can't leave everything
       like that. Mark? Ring me.

Scene 3.

*[Rather than the entire message on Mark's machine, we hear
just the tone, then:]*

BETH   Mark, it's Beth again. Where are you? I'm
       desperate. We have to talk. The more I think
       about it, the more depressed I feel. Pick up the
       phone. *[Sighs]*

Scene 4.

*[Rather than the entire message on Mark's machine, we hear
just the tone, then:]*

BETH   It's Beth, Mark, and I... I'm sorry to be such a
       pain in the neck. But I feel so bad and... I can't

stand the idea that it's over. You know? I...I
need to talk to you about last night. If you
don't ring back soon, I'll...I don't know what
I'll do. Ring me, Mark. Ring me.

Scene 5.

[Rather than the entire message on Mark's machine, we hear just the tone, then:]

DEREK   Mark, pick up the phone if you're there. It's
Derek. Pick up the piggin' phone. Look, Beth
just phoned. She sounded really upset. I don't
know what's going on, but...I'm worried about
her. So ring me *now*.

Scene 6.

[Rather than the entire message on Mark's machine, we hear just the tone, then:]

BETH   *[With great peace]* Mark. Hi, it's me again. I feel
much better now. Sorry about all those other
messages.

Scene 7.

[Rather than the entire message on Mark's machine, we hear just the tone, then:]

DEREK   Mark, it's Derek. I'm at the University Hospital.
The emergency room. You need to get down
here right away. Do you hear me? I went to see
Beth and she...took an overdose of something.
I don't know what. Get down here.

Scene 8.

[Mark's room/apartment. He enters as if just returning from a trip. He drops an overnight bag on the floor, looks around, sees the answering machine on a stand nearby and punches the play button while he checks his mail. It clicks, beeps and then:]

ANSWERING MACHINE VOICE   You have eight messages. I will
play messages.

[The machine clicks and beeps:]

BETH   Mark, are you there? Pick up the phone. Come
on, we need to talk. Mark! *[Sighs]* Okay, fine.
Ring me.

*[He growls at her while he opens his mail. The first message
finishes and the machine clicks, beeps and the second
message begins.]*

BETH   Mark... pick up the phone if you're there.
Seriously. I'm really... *[Beat]* Look, we need to
talk about last night. We can't leave everything
like that. Mark? Ring me.

*[This message brings him away from the mail and to the
machine to turn it off.]*

MARK   No way. I'm not interested. *[Shouts at the
machine]* Do you hear me, Beth? I'm *not*
interested!

[Derek enters. He's a bit agitated.]

DEREK   What are you doing? Where in the world have
you been?

MARK   I'm having a bonding experience with my
answering machine. Do you see that light – the
way it's flashing?

DEREK   What about it?

MARK   That tells me I have *a lot* of messages waiting
for me. And do you know who they're from?
They're all from *Beth*.

DEREK   Not all of them, actually.

MARK   Oh – you wanna bet? They're all her. I can tell
by the annoying, *demanding* way the light is

flashing. Why did I ever start going out with her?

DEREK   I believe at the time you said she was beautiful, intelligent, and perfect for you.

MARK   You're my best friend, why didn't you stop me?

DEREK   Look, Mark –

MARK   You don't know what it's been like. Did you see *Play Misty for Me* with Clint Eastwood? Psycho-broad chases him around and tries to kill him. Remember *Fatal Attraction*? That's what I'm dealing with here.

DEREK   Really?

MARK   We go out a few times, enjoy ourselves a little and the next thing I know, she's got all kinds of expectations.

DEREK   You've been going out for six months.

MARK   Amazing, isn't it? Man, that's why I had to get out of here.

DEREK   *[Nudges overnight bag with his foot]* You left.

MARK   I certainly did. After last night, I knew what she'd do. The phone would ring and I'd go mad. So I drove over to Jimmy's.

DEREK   'After last night...' What's that mean?

MARK   We went out and I told her I couldn't take all the emotional blackmail anymore. You know what I'm talking about.

DEREK   I don't remember emotional blackmail. I thought you got along well.

MARK   Ha. You have no idea. You only saw her when

we were together in public. But behind closed doors...

DEREK   Behind closed doors – what?

MARK   She was different. She made me feel... trapped. That's it. Trapped. Where do women get these expectations? – that's what I want to know. Not from me.

DEREK   What are you talking about – expectations?

MARK   You know, that I'll only go out with her and I'll ring her all the time and... things like that. It's as if her talons were digging in my skin and I had no freedom. Why do women get like that? You'd think I told her that I loved her or something.

DEREK   Did you?

MARK   Well, no. I don't think I ever came right out and *said* 'I love you.' I said, 'I *think* I could love you.' *Big* difference.

DEREK   To you or to her?

MARK   What's it matter? I didn't actually say the words, but she got the idea anyway. I should've seen it coming. That look in her eye. I've seen it before.

DEREK   Look in her eye? What kind of look?

MARK   You know – that soft, wet, melted kind of look. We're laying there and she turns to me with that look and –

DEREK   Hold on. 'Laying there'. What do you mean?

MARK   What do you mean, what do I mean?

DEREK   You mean you two...

MARK   Well...

DEREK   You slept with her.

MARK   Only a couple of times.

DEREK   A couple of times.

MARK   A week.

DEREK   A couple of times a week!

MARK   Not *every* week. Only after the first couple of
            months. What's with you?

DEREK   I think this story just took a dramatic turn.

MARK   What are you talking about?

DEREK   You *slept* with her – and you wonder why she
            had expectations?

MARK   Hey – it's not like that. She asked for it... she
            seduced me.

DEREK   What? *Beth*? How – by not saying no when you
            kissed her on the first date?

MARK   Well, yeah. I mean, that's how it works right?
            You get closer and closer and... why am I
            talking to you about this? It's over.

DEREK   What is?

MARK   My relationship with Beth. It's over. That's what
            happened last night. I said I was tired of the
            emotional baggage and all her expectations and
            that we were through.

DEREK   You slept with her and then you dumped her. Is
            that what you're telling me?

MARK   'Dumped her' is a very callous way to put it. I
            didn't *dump* her. I just... terminated our
            ongoing relationship.

DEREK   You dumped her. Well, thank you. That explains a lot.

MARK   I know that tone in your voice. You're gonna take an attitude with me. Don't forget what happened to you and Rachel.

DEREK   Bringing up Rachel doesn't mean you get let off the hook. Rachel didn't wind up in the hospital.

MARK   Oh, right. As if Beth did.

DEREK   She did. That's why I'm here, you fool.

MARK   What're you talking about?

DEREK   She overdosed on some pills. Why she thought *you* were important to get so upset over is beyond me, but there you are.

MARK   What? Overdosed! Tell me you're lying.

DEREK   It's the truth.

MARK   *[Pause, as it sinks in]* Oh… just like *Fatal Attraction.*

DEREK   Will you drop the movie analogies? This is real life. And we're not dealing with a 'psycho-broad' here, Mark. We're talking about *Beth* – a very sweet girl who deserved better than she got.

MARK   I better go see her.

DEREK   That's not such a good idea.

MARK   Why not?

DEREK   Because she's calm now. She realised she did a very stupid thing. Seeing you might… might make her wanna kill herself for being suicidal.

MARK   I don't believe this. What was she thinking?

DEREK   What *was* she thinking? Well, call me a fussy
            old traditionalist, but I believe she thought you
            loved her.

MARK   But I never said... I mean...

DEREK   Maybe you never said the *words*, Mark. But
            since when are words the be-all and end-all of
            how we say things to each other? It's what we
            do. That's what tells people where we are or
            who we are or... what we stand for.

MARK   Look, I won't be made the bad guy here. I
            won't. All right, maybe I gave her the wrong
            impression. But I can't help it if she got carried
            away. That's not my fault. *[Pause/beat]* Is she all
            right? I mean, she's not going to die or
            anything, right?

DEREK   She's all right. In fact, I think she has a date
            with the doctor who pumped her stomach.

MARK   What? You're pulling my leg. She wouldn't do
            that.

DEREK   How do you know? Psycho-broads are liable to
            do anything.

*[Mark sits down, lost in his own thoughts. Obviously he feels
bad.]*

DEREK   I think... I think we kid ourselves when we stop
            believing that what we do means something –
            to someone – all the time. We speak volumes to
            each other without ever opening our mouths.
            That's why... it's why we have to be
            careful... and do the right thing. *[Beat]* I really
            didn't come over to lecture you. I only wanted
            you to know what happened to Beth. That's all.
            [He makes as if to go] Listen to the rest of the
            messages, all right?

[Mark doesn't respond, Derek exits. Mark then gets up and punches the button on the machine. It resume where we left off. He sits down and listens to the drama unfold with great emotion.]

BETH   Mark, it's Beth again. Where are you? I'm desperate. We have to talk. The more I think about it, the more depressed I feel. Pick up the phone. *[Sighs]*

BETH   It's Beth, Mark, and I... I'm sorry to be such a pain in the neck. But I feel so bad and... I can't stand the idea that it's over. You know? I... I need to talk to you about last night. If you don't ring back soon, I'll... I don't know what I'll do. Ring me, Mark. Ring me.

DEREK   Mark, pick up the phone if you're there. It's Derek. Pick up the bloody phone. Look, Beth just phoned. She sounded really upset. I don't know what's going on, but... I'm worried about her. So ring me *now*.

BETH   *[With great peace]* Mark. Hi, it's me again. I feel much better now. Sorry about all those other messages.

DEREK   Mark, it's Derek. I'm at the University Hospital. The emergency room. You need to get down here right away. Do you hear me? I went to see Beth and she... took an overdose of something. I don't know what. Get down here.

[And then... a message we haven't heard, after the tone.]

BETH   *[Wearily]* Mark? It's me, Beth. I think Derek is coming to see you. I tried to stop him, but... I'm sorry about all this. It was a really stupid thing to do. It's only that... I never, you know, gave myself to anyone like that before... But I did – for you – because I thought... The way

you acted... I thought... well, whatever I
thought, I was wrong. I see that now. *[Pause]*
Don't feel bad, if you do. I was stupid for
believing that you... I was stupid for
believing... *[She sighs deeply]*

*[She hangs up and the dial tone comes on, then cuts itself off.
The 'machine voice' comes on and says:]*

ANSWERING MACHINE VOICE   End of message...

[Mark grabs his jacket and exits.]

Blackout. [Curtain.]

23. Three strands

In which a father and daughter reunite under difficult circumstances.

Theme
Forgiveness and reconciliation.

Characters
Dr Pendleton.
Diana – the long-suffering daughter.
George – the estranged father.

Setting
A hospital waiting room.

[Dr Pendleton enters, obviously speaking to someone off-stage. Diana enters, spots him in his uniform, and approaches.]

DR PENDLETON　Yeah – *[waves them off]* I'll see you later. *[Beat]* Right. You have a good weekend, too.

DIANA　Dr Pendleton?

DR PENDLETON　Uh huh.

DIANA　The nurse said I'd find you in here. I'm Diana Fisk. I'm here about Tom.

DR PENDLETON　*[Shakes her hand]* Oh yes. We spoke on the phone earlier.

DIANA　That's right.

DR PENDLETON　Do you want to go see him now?

DIANA　Well, that's hard to say. I rang my father and thought I should wait until he gets here.

DR PENDLETON　I'm sure Tom will be glad to see the two of you.

DIANA　The shock might kill him. We haven't seen each other in – oh, a long time, to be specific.

DR PENDLETON　You're not a close family?

DIANA　Depends on what you mean by 'close'. What was 'close' in my family is called 'domestic violence' in others. It was like that even before our parents divorced. Tom and I went with my mother but she died last year and... *[Shrugs]* It doesn't matter. My father probably won't come

anyway. He was surprised when I told
him.

DR PENDLETON   You mean he didn't know about Tom's
condition until today?

DIANA   I suppose that was my fault. I simply
couldn't figure out how to tell him. My
father isn't very patient about things like
this – y'know, getting sick, dying. He
thinks it's a sign of weakness. I'm not
terribly keen on it myself, to be honest.
That's why I haven't... until you called...
Does he look bad?

DR PENDLETON   Brace yourself. Yes.

DIANA   My father isn't going to like it.

DR PENDLETON   Tom's not thrilled either.

DIANA   But I know what my father'll say. He'll
say that Tom should've been more clever.
He thinks if you're clever, take care of
yourself, you won't die.

DR PENDLETON   As a doctor, I can assure you I've met a
lot of very clever people who became very
sick.

DIANA   You don't have to tell me.

DR PENDLETON   [Looks at watch] You'll have to forgive me,
Diana, but I have to go.

DIANA   [Anxiously] You do? But – what if we have
questions or... something happens?

DR PENDLETON   I'm not Tom's regular doctor. I was filling
in this week while Dr Edwards was at a
conference. He should be back within the
hour.

DIANA	But –
DR PENDLETON	Dr Edwards is particularly good with this sort of thing.
DIANA	Right. Yeah. Dr Edwards is probably better looking than you anyway.
DR PENDLETON	Right. *[Shakes her hand]* Just… brace yourself. And try not to upset him.
DIANA	*I* won't. But I can't speak for my father.
DR PENDLETON	Thanks. Goodbye. *[He exits]*
DIANA	Bye. *[When it's clear the doctor's gone, Diana paces nervously]* I'm just not sure what's worse: waiting to see Tom or waiting for Dad. *[Spots a coffee machine]* A cup of coffee is what I need. That'll calm me down. *[Moves to get some coffee, hums nervously as she does]* Maybe I should phone Dad and tell him not to come. It'll just upset Tommy and make my stomach go all squirty. *[Beat]* But if he's dying, then they should see each other. I don't know why – but it seems like the right thing to do. *[Beat]* I wonder if there's a phone around here? I'll phone him and tell him… *[Beat]* Nah. If he comes, he comes. If not, then it's his loss. *[Beat]* I'll phone. I won't give him a choice. I'll tell him he has to come. This is no time to be a stubborn old –

[George, the father, enters.]

GEORGE	Where have you been?
DIANA	Dad!
GEORGE	I've been downstairs in the lobby for ten

minutes. You didn't say to meet you up here.

DIANA   I thought that –

GEORGE   I came *this* close to going home. You know I don't like hospitals. I stood in that obnoxious flower shop looking at sympathy cards. You know I hate sympathy cards.

DIANA   I know.

GEORGE   Don't just stand there looking at me like a fish at feeding time.

DIANA   I knew this was a bad idea. Tommy's gonna throw his bedpan at us and die.

GEORGE   So is he in a special ward or something?

DIANA   I don't know.

GEORGE   Well, what *do* you know?

DIANA   Nothing. The doctor said to brace ourselves.

GEORGE   For what?

DIANA   For how he looks, I guess.

GEORGE   What does that mean? He *never* looked very good.

DIANA   I think the doctor was talking about the illness.

GEORGE   Oh that. It's his own fault. He never took care of himself. *[Beat]* You're not going to cry are you?

DIANA   No!

GEORGE	I know how you get and your blubbering isn't going to help anything.
DIANA	I won't blubber.
GEORGE	Good. Why did you wait so long to phone? You should've called me before this.
DIANA	I should have, but – I knew it would make you mad.
GEORGE	Mad! He'll be lucky if I talk to him at all. How long has he been in here?
DIANA	I'm not sure. I only found out a few weeks ago because Kevin called and told me.
GEORGE	Kevin. You mean my nephew Kevin?
DIANA	Uh huh.
GEORGE	Why'd he phone you? Why didn't he phone me?
DIANA	Because he hates you. Most of the family hates you.
GEORGE	That's because I wouldn't pamper you lot. Your mother's side of the family spoiled all of you. So – when did he ring you? A month ago? Six weeks?
DIANA	Three weeks.
GEORGE	Three weeks. You should've called me sooner. Why didn't you phone me?
DIANA	Because I didn't want you to come marching down here and lecture him about getting sick.
GEORGE	Give me a little credit.

DIANA	You would have.
GEORGE	Well, I'm his father. I'm supposed to lecture my children.
DIANA	Not this time.
GEORGE	He brought it on himself – the pencil pusher. If he listened to me and took care of himself, this wouldn't have happened.
DIANA	Maybe not, but there's no point in telling him now.
GEORGE	Do you want to write down what I should and shouldn't say?
DIANA	No, I'm only telling you –
GEORGE	I know what you're telling me. You're telling me that you think I'm an insensitive clod who won't handle the situation very well.
DIANA	The doctor told me that we shouldn't upset him.
GEORGE	What about *him* upsetting *us*? It's just like him to do this.
DIANA	What? Get sick and die?
GEORGE	Anything for attention.
DIANA	Just mind yourself, all right?
GEORGE	Don't tell me to mind myself. I'll mind whatever I have a mind to mind.
DIANA	Forget it. I can't do this. I knew it was a mistake.
GEORGE	What now?
DIANA	I can't go in to see him. Not with you.

GEORGE	Why not?
DIANA	Because we're out here fighting and I don't want it to happen in there.
GEORGE	You think this is a fight? This is no fight.
DIANA	It's close enough for me.
GEORGE	You were always the sensitive one.
DIANA	So what?
GEORGE	Tom and I would get to wrestling around and you'd scream like a baby.
DIANA	That's because I *was* a baby. I thought you two were killing each other.
GEORGE	Why're you so tense?
DIANA	*[Surprised]* How can you ask me that question? Look at where we are, think about what we're doing.
GEORGE	We're in a hospital! I'm the one who hates them, not you.
DIANA	I may be seeing my brother for the last time! This could be – Oh, never mind.
GEORGE	What?
DIANA	What what?
GEORGE	I mean, what in the world are you talking about? Can we go in and see him now?
DIANA	No. I'm not ready yet. *[Beat]* Do you know what? Sometimes I think… I mean it's like we aren't even related. An accident at birth, switched cradles. Tom's in there dying, I'm racked with guilt, and you're acting like – like –

GEORGE   Like what?

DIANA   Like we interrupted Match of the Day.
            How did we survive?

GEORGE   We didn't. Your mother took you away
            from me.

DIANA   You didn't want us anyway.

GEORGE   I didn't know what to do with you. I
            never did.

DIANA   That says it all.

GEORGE   What?

DIANA   No wonder we've hardly spoken.

GEORGE   You're only now figuring this out?

DIANA   It's not right.

GEORGE   It's the way it is.

DIANA   We're family.

GEORGE   So?

DIANA   So, that should mean something. Hasn't
            it ever bothered you? The distance?

GEORGE   I thought if you wanted to talk, you'd
            phone.

DIANA   And what if I thought that if you wanted
            to talk, *you'd* phone *me*?

GEORGE   Then I assume our phones wouldn't be
            ringing very much. You like to talk more
            than I do anyway.

DIANA   And Tommy – his phone wasn't ringing
            very much either.

GEORGE   I'm not going to feel guilty about that.

DIANA   You don't feel guilty about anything.

GEORGE   Why should I? Being family doesn't mean
             we have to coddle each other day in and
             day out. I'm your father, not your
             nursemaid. We live out our lives with no
             false illusions about familial
             responsibilities and obligations.

DIANA   I have no idea what you just said.

GEORGE   I think you get my meaning.

DIANA   No. I don't. *I'm* talking about the distance
             between you and me and Tommy. What
             were *you* talking about?

GEORGE   I'm talking about choices. We all made
             our choices. I'm not gonna get
             sentimental simply because one of us is
             sick.

DIANA   Dying.

GEORGE   That's his choice, too. If he took care of
             himself like I said –

DIANA   But don't you think we might've made
             different choices if... if we stayed close...
             Maybe if we showed each other love
             instead of... of nothing? Don't you ever
             wish things could've been different?
             Maybe –

GEORGE   Maybe this, maybe that. Who knows?
             You expect too much. We're just family.
             The same as always. It was your Mother
             who took care of all the details.

DIANA   Details? You mean, like showing *love*?
             Those kinds of details?

GEORGE   Sure. If you want to blame anyone, blame

her for dying first. She was the one with the heart in our family. She was the one who... *[Beat, impatiently]* You talk too much. You always have. Can we go in now?

DIANA   But you're my father. Don't we love each other?

GEORGE   I haven't thought about it. You see? You think too much and you talk too much.

DIANA   Can't we look beyond our differences?

GEORGE   I never had a reason to try.

DIANA   We have a reason now, don't we?

GEORGE   I knew it was gonna get to this point. You want to have a big emotional moment and you're going to cry. I knew it.

DIANA   I am not. But I can't help wondering... Is it too late?

GEORGE   Too late for what?

DIANA   To try to be... family.

GEORGE   You must be joking.

DIANA   No. Can't we do it?

GEORGE   After all these years you want me to act like your father? I'm too old.

DIANA   You were too *young* for it before... and now you're too old? When's the right age, the right time? You could be in there dying and who'd come to see you? Everyone hates you.

GEORGE   But they *respect* me – and they'll come

	because they'll feel guilty otherwise. And they don't want to be left out of my will.
DIANA	Will! A bottle cap collection and a '74 Morris Minor?
GEORGE	And the bird houses.
DIANA	Oh yes. Bird houses made out of toothpicks. *[Pause/beat]* What did I ever do to you?
GEORGE	You didn't do *anything*. What are you harping about?
DIANA	*[Pause]* Dad... what if... if I asked you to forgive me.
GEORGE	Forgive you! Forgive you for *what*? What have you done to me since you used my best ties as belts?
DIANA	Nothing. That's the point. I've been a stranger. Certainly not your daughter.
GEORGE	You're getting yourself worked up.
DIANA	You're right. I am. Because I want to ask Tommy for forgiveness, too. For not being the sister I should've been. Maybe I can try to be – in whatever time is left.
GEORGE	There won't be much time if you keep standing out here rabbiting on.
DIANA	If I asked, will you forgive me?
GEORGE	Those ties went out of style a long time ago.
DIANA	Will you forgive me?
GEORGE	*[Pause]* Depends on whether you mean it

or not – and if I have to say the same thing back. Do you mean it?

DIANA   Yeah, I mean it.

GEORGE   *[Shrugs]* Okay. Consider yourself forgiven – if it'll make you feel better.

DIANA   This isn't to make me feel better.

GEORGE   Well, it's not doing anything for *me*. *[Quickly]* And don't think I'm going to jump on this little emotional bandwagon and ask *you* for forgiveness. I didn't do anything wrong. You and your brother left with your mother. We were different, we went our separate ways, why does it have to be a big deal? Why do you have to get like this? Next you'll be blubbing and reciting poetry and expecting us to hug.

DIANA   Forget about it.

GEORGE   And if you think I'm going in there and ask *Tommy* for forgiveness, you've got another thing coming. I was a *good* father to him when he was little. I showed him things, taught him, spent time with him. *He* was the one who turned on *me*, the little ingrate. He was the one who went with your mother and suddenly decided he was above all the things we used to do. He was the one who got high and mighty – *[stops himself, surprised]* This is stupid.

DIANA   High and mighty? *Our* Tommy?

GEORGE   Yes. When your mother left. He could have stayed with me.

DIANA   What?

GEORGE   Right. You were too young. The solicitors
             were clear about that. You had to go with
             your mother. But Tommy... he was old
             enough to choose for himself.

DIANA   Is that what this is all about? The choice
             he made then? He was ten years old!

GEORGE   It's the principle of the thing.

DIANA   Dad, did you ever talk to Tommy about
             this?

GEORGE   There was nothing to say.

DIANA   There was *plenty* to say. You've been
             chewing on it all these years.

GEORGE   I haven't given it a minute's thought.

DIANA   I could understand how you and I drifted
             apart – but you and Tommy, it never
             made sense until now. You think he
             decided against you. But he didn't. He
             was certain that *you* didn't want *him*.

GEORGE   Don't be absurd.

DIANA   Did you ever say? Did you ever tell him
             you wanted him to live with you?

GEORGE   Why should I have to say such a thing to
             my own son? He should know.

DIANA   *[Sadly]* He didn't. He thought you didn't
             want him. Just like *I* thought you didn't
             want me. Oh, Dad... what have we done?

GEORGE   *[Pause]* I didn't do anything.

DIANA   That's right. You did *nothing*.

GEORGE   Don't get preachy.

DIANA   Call it what you want. All I know is that
               my brother – and your son – is dying and
               we've lost so much time. Then it's just
               going to be the two of us – and we don't
               know each other. Can we get to know
               each other again, Dad? Is it possible? Can
               we… start over?

GEORGE   This is that emotional moment I was
               talking about. You're going to cry.

DIANA   Shut up, will you? Can we?

GEORGE   I don't know.

DIANA   Can we *try*?

GEORGE   *[Pause, shrugs]* Yeah. I suppose we can try.

DIANA   Thank you.

GEORGE   Can we go see Tom now – or would you
               rather stay out here and have another
               emotional moment while he passes on?

DIANA   *[Pause]* Yeah. Okay. We can go in. *[As a
               directive]* But we go in as his family.

[George rolls his eyes, then nods.]

GEORGE   Yeah, yeah – family.

[They move as if to exit.]

GEORGE   You're such an idiot. We were never *not*
               family, you know. I mean, maybe we
               weren't *good* family – but I never felt like
               you and Tom weren't my children any
               more.

DIANA   It would've been nice if you said so once
               in a while.

GEORGE   You talk too much. Let's go.

DIANA   *[At the edge of the stage, Diana stops]* Wait.

GEORGE   What?

DIANA   I can't do it. I can't go in.

GEORGE   What are you talking about? Of course you can.

DIANA   I can't. I'm scared. You go ahead.

GEORGE   Not a chance. You're coming with me.

DIANA   I *can't*! I'm too scared. I can't see him like this.

GEORGE   I knew you'd cry. Look, I'm here. *[Puts his arm around her]*

DIANA   *[Grabs George in a half-hug]* Dad –

GEORGE   Take it easy, Diana. It's all right.

DIANA   Dad.

[The half-hug becomes a full hug between them.]

GEORGE   It's all right. We'll go in together. All right? *[Puts his arms on Diana's shoulders to face her]* All right?

DIANA   *[Collecting herself]* Right. Together.

GEORGE   Together.

[With his arm still around Diana, George leads them out.]

Blackout. [Curtain.]

24. A pilgrim's prayer

In which we use the style of Bunyan's classic Pilgrim's Progress *to learn about prayer.*

Theme
Prayer.

Characters
Narrator One.
Narrator Two.
Christian.
IMeMine.
Rules Verne.
Christiana.
Elijah.

Setting
On the road to find out.

Note
This sketch is written for presentation to children.

[Scene opens with our two narrators positioned on opposite sides of the stage. They begin...]

NARRATOR ONE   This is a story.

NARRATOR TWO   But not like any story.

NARRATOR ONE   It's a story about you – and me.

NARRATOR TWO   But since we can't all fit on the stage, let's say it's a story about you and me as found in a young man named *Christian*.

[Christian enters, wandering casually.]

NARRATOR ONE   Christian was an all-round nice person, but lately he wasn't very happy.

[Christian reflects this by slumping sadly.]

NARRATOR TWO   He felt like something was missing in his life.

NARRATOR ONE   In his *heart*.

NARRATOR TWO   And he wasn't sure what the problem was.

NARRATOR ONE   Until one day he wandered into his parents' library at home.

[Christian wanders into library.]

NARRATOR TWO   His parents loved to read, you see, and had a library filled with books.

NARRATOR ONE   But there was one very special book that caught Christian's eye.

[Christian sees a book and pulls it off the shelf curiously. He opens it and begins to read as the narration continues.]

CHRISTIAN   Cool.

NARRATOR TWO   He read the book again and again.

NARRATOR ONE   And became happy once more.

NARRATOR TWO   Because the book was filled with stories about God and the relationship he had with the people who loved him.

NARRATOR ONE	It talked about all the things God did for them.
NARRATOR TWO	And how he gave them wonderful things.
NARRATOR ONE	And talked to them.
NARRATOR TWO	And He –
CHRISTIAN	Wait a minute. Hold it. These stories are great, but I wanna talk to God myself. I mean, if these people can do it, why can't I?
NARRATOR ONE	And so Christian decided to learn how to talk to God.
CHRISTIAN	*[Kneels]* God, I know you are good and that you love me, so please teach me how to talk to You.

[IMeMine approaches as Christian prays.]

IMEMINE	Hey, you.
CHRISTIAN	Yes?
IMEMINE	You're going about this all wrong. You wanna pray right?
CHRISTIAN	Sure.
IMEMINE	Then you have to stop this namby-pamby *please* stuff. You have to pray like I do. You say confidently and boldly: 'Hey, God, if you really love me you'll give me what I want!'
CHRISTIAN	That's how you pray?
IMEMINE	Yeah. It works for me every time! And it'll work for you, too – or my name isn't IMeMine *[pronounced: 'I-Me-Mine']*.
CHRISTIAN	IMeMine?

IMEMINE   Did I stutter?

CHRISTIAN   No.

IMEMINE   Pray like that and tell him what you want
               and – bingo – it's yours.

CHRISTIAN   Thanks! I'll try it!

[IMeMine exits as Christian prays.]

CHRISTIAN   Hey, God – *[self-consciously, not meaning to
               be disrespectful]* – uh, *Lord* – if you really
               love me you'll give me what I want. And I
               want a... uh...

[Christian turns to audience.]

CHRISTIAN   What should I ask for?

*[Hopefully the audience will respond with suggestions and
Christian picks one to ask for – marked from this point on
with an X.]*

CHRISTIAN   Hey, God, if you really love me you'll give
               me what I want – and I want a X.

*[Christian waits for a moment, as if hoping his request will
be granted immediately. As he continues, Rules Verne enters
and watches Christian with bemusement.]*

CHRISTIAN   I said, I want a X! *[Beat]* Uh, please? *[Beat]*
               Hello? Hello! Are you listening? Hello?

RULES VERNE   Hello.

CHRISTIAN   *[Thinking it's God]* Oh, hello. Now we're
               getting somewhere. I was saying that I
               would like a X.

RULES VERNE   Well, you're not going to get it wandering
               around shouting on an unrealistic-
               looking stage.

CHRISTIAN   *[Turns to Rules Verne]* Oh – sorry. I

thought you were – never mind. Who are you?

RULES VERNE   The name is Rules Verne and I know exactly what you thought. And it won't work, you know. Simply asking God for things isn't good enough. He's not a genie. It's not like you can make three wishes and *presto-chango* he'll give them to you.

CHRISTIAN   He won't?

RULES VERNE   There's a lot more to it than that. There are things you have to *do* to get God's attention.

CHRISTIAN   Do? Like what?

RULES VERNE   Any number of things. Like kneeling. Go on.

CHRISTIAN   *[Kneeling]* Okay.

RULES VERNE   Then you might try lifting your hands up in the air.

CHRISTIAN   *[Lifting hands]* Right.

RULES VERNE   Maybe you might smile up to God.

CHRISTIAN   *[Smiles upwards]* Smiling.

RULES VERNE   But you don't want to act as if you're being silly, so perhaps you should have a pleading look in your eyes.

CHRISTIAN   *[Pleading eyes]* Pleading. How's that?

RULES VERNE   *[Ponders Christian]* Awful. You may want to change your clothes, too.

CHRISTIAN   And then God'll answer my prayers.

RULES VERNE   Perhaps. It depends on how long you pray.

CHRISTIAN   How long I pray?

RULES VERNE   Yes. The longer, the better your chances. *[Pats Christian encouragingly]* I'll let you get to it.

CHRISTIAN   Thanks.

RULES VERNE   *[Exiting]* Remember: the longer the better.

[Christian nods and stays in that position.]

CHRISTIAN   An hour. I'll pray for an hour.

[Christian's eyes get heavy almost immediately as the narration begins again.]

NARRATOR ONE   Christian's plan to pray for a whole hour met with one tiny problem.

NARRATOR TWO   He fell asleep after the first ten seconds.

[Christian slumps into slumber.]

NARRATOR ONE   And as he slept, his sister – named Christiana –

[Christiana enters, stops when she sees Christian.]

NARRATOR ONE   – came into the room.

CHRISTIANA   *[Gently waking Christian]* Christian? Christian?

[Christian suddenly snaps back into his 'prayer' position.]

CHRISTIAN   *Ipso facto, magna carta!* Amen!

CHRISTIANA   Christian, what were you doing?

CHRISTIAN   Praying! (Sort of.)

CHRISTIANA   It looked like you were sleeping to me.

CHRISTIAN   You'd sleep, too, if you prayed for as long as I did.

CHRISTIANA   How long did you pray?

CHRISTIAN   Ten... *[sadly]* seconds. I wanted to pray for an hour but didn't make it.

CHRISTIANA   You wanted to pray for a whole *hour*?

CHRISTIAN   Yeah. But I fell asleep. I'm a failure.

CHRISTIANA   Why didn't you try to pray for thirty seconds first, or maybe a minute.

CHRISTIAN   A minute! You can't pray for a minute.

CHRISTIANA   Why not?

CHRISTIAN   Well... because.

CHRISTIANA   All right – do me a favour and run down to the store for me.

CHRISTIAN   Run to the store! You're kidding. That's five miles from here.

CHRISTIANA   You can't run that far?

CHRISTIAN   No.

CHRISTIANA   Then how about doing one hundred press-ups and *then* running to the store for me?

CHRISTIAN   You're crazy.

CHRISTIANA   Why?

CHRISTIAN   Because I can't do a hundred press-ups any more than I can run five miles. You know that.

CHRISTIANA   Right. You can't run five miles because you haven't trained to run five miles. You can't do a hundred press-ups because you haven't trained to do a hundred press-ups. So why did you think you could pray for an entire hour? Praying is a discipline – it's sort of like exercising – and you have to keep doing it. Where in the world are you getting your ideas?

CHRISTIAN   Well, Rules Verne said I needed to pray in a certain position for a long time in order to make God give me what I want.

CHRISTIANA   To *make* God give you what you want?

CHRISTIAN   Yeah. Something wrong?

CHRISTIANA   I never thought I could *make* God do anything.

CHRISTIAN   But if he loves me, he'll give me what I want.

CHRISTIANA   Mum and Dad love you, right?

CHRISTIAN   I think so.

CHRISTIANA   You know so. And they don't give you everything you want no matter *how* you ask them.

CHRISTIAN   You can say that again.

CHRISTIANA   Why don't they?

CHRISTIAN   Because they're cruel?

CHRISTIANA   No. Because they love you – and not everything you want is good for you. God's the same way. Because he's your heavenly father and loves you, he's not going to give you anything and everything just because you ask. What kind of father would he be if he did that?

CHRISTIAN	But what's the use of praying if God doesn't answer?
CHRISTIANA	God *does* answer – but not always in ways we expect. And that reminds me of a story. Sit down.

[They sit down – off to one side of the stage.]

| NARRATOR TWO | So Christiana told Christian a story about a man named Elijah – |

[Man steps forward.]

ELIJAH	That's me.
NARRATOR TWO	– who was a great prophet of God.
ELIJAH	*[Modestly]* Well, I don't know about *great*.
NARRATOR TWO	The man did wondrous works for God.
ELIJAH	Only one or two.
NARRATOR ONE	He even challenged the false prophets who worshipped false gods to an amazing challenge – and showed them to be the liars and fakes they were by bringing down fire from heaven.
ELIJAH	Anyone could have done it, really.
NARRATOR TWO	And when he finished doing that, he called rain from heaven and ended a three-year drought.
ELIJAH	And that can be pretty tiring, let me tell you.
NARRATOR ONE	Worn-out and lonely, he went off to the mountains to consult with God, praying for help and strength. And God told him to listen.
ELIJAH	I'm listening.

NARRATOR TWO   Suddenly a mighty windstorm hit the mountain.

[Some of your actors, making all the noise of a windstorm, should come 'swirling' around Elijah. He braces himself against them.]

NARRATOR ONE   It was such a terrible blast that the rocks were torn loose.

ELIJAH   All right, God, you have my attention!

[The windstorm exits. Elijah looks around.]

NARRATOR TWO   But God was not in the windstorm.

ELIJAH   I wonder where he is, then.

NARRATOR ONE   And then an earthquake came!

[Elijah bounces around as some of your actors, making earthquake noises, bounce across the stage.]

NARRATOR TWO   It shook and rattled and rolled.

ELIJAH   I'm listening, God!

[The earthquake exits. Elijah looks around.]

NARRATOR ONE   But God was not in the earthquake.

NARRATOR TWO   And then there was a great fire!

[Your actors, waving their arms like flames and making crackling noises, rush around Elijah.]

ELIJAH   This has to be the message. Go ahead, God, I'm listening!

[The fire exits. Elijah pats himself as if he might be smouldering.]

ELIJAH   *[Coughs]* Well?

NARRATOR ONE   But God was not in the fire.

ELIJAH   I give up.

NARRATOR TWO   Just then there was the sound of a gentle whisper, like a still, small voice.

ELIJAH   *[Cocks his head to hear]* Is that you, Lord?

NARRATOR ONE   And it was.

[Elijah kneels down to pray and listen.]

CHRISTIAN   I don't get it.

CHRISTIANA   God doesn't always do big, spectacular things to speak to us. Sometimes he speaks in ways we don't expect.

CHRISTIAN   Oh. Well, Christiana, since you have this all sorted out – maybe we should try praying together.

CHRISTIANA   All right...

[They both kneel.]

NARRATOR ONE   And they both knelt down together.

NARRATOR TWO   And after a minute...

CHRISTIAN   You go first.

CHRISTIANA   Why should I go first? You go first.

CHRISTIAN   You're the prayer expert. You go first.

CHRISTIANA   I'm not used to praying with someone else. Go ahead.

CHRISTIAN   No, you go. I don't know what to say.

NARRATOR ONE   On and on it went until Christian – who seemed to have a knack for such things – spied another book.

CHRISTIAN   *[Picking up a book]* Hey, look.

CHRISTIANA   It's a prayer book!

NARRATOR TWO   They opened the prayer book and found just the right words to help them pray.

CHRISTIAN & CHRISTIANA
Our Father, who art in heaven, hallowed be thy name...

[They bow their heads as the narration continues.]

NARRATOR ONE   Soon they realised they were on to a good thing and they invited others to join them to pray.

[Other cast members enter and kneel next to Christian and Christiana.]

NARRATOR TWO   And together they discovered that prayer is a process that is practised and learned – especially when people do it together.

NARRATOR ONE   But most important: it's just one part of a relationship with the God who loves them and likes to hear from them.

NARRATOR TWO   So you see? This story was about you and me after all.

NARRATOR ONE   May we all live happily ever after.

NARRATOR TWO   Amen.

[The cast exit.]

Blackout. [Curtain.]

25. In a nutshell

In which we get: A History Of The Church In One Act

Theme
The church, for better or worse.

Characters
Justin.
Simon.

Setting
Throughout history.

Note
Though this was originally written for two performers,
you may want to expand the roles for more than that.

[The stage is simple: chairs sit in the middle while, off to both sides, sit two small desks where, at various times, our two characters will retreat to deal with important matters. Simon and Justin enter from opposite sides of the stage, turn to the audience and look as if they're listening to the final words of Jesus before the ascension. Then their eyes drift upwards as Jesus ascends. Simon clasps his hands reverently. Justin waves.]

JUSTIN   Bye, Lord. See you again soon – we hope.

SIMON   *Very* soon, I expect.

JUSTIN   *[Sighs contentedly, speaks to Simon]* He's gone.

SIMON   I wonder what we're supposed to do now.

[Suddenly they both look as if they've been jabbed with a cattle prod – or a vision – their faces alive.]

SIMON   I think I just had a vision.

JUSTIN   So did I.

SIMON   That's amazing.

JUSTIN   Do you know what I want to do? I want to proclaim Jesus in the streets!

SIMON   In the languages of the people – so they'll understand the good news!

JUSTIN   And I want to sell everything I own!

SIMON   And share it all with other believers!

JUSTIN   And help the poor and orphans!

SIMON   And widows!

JUSTIN   And die for my faith.

SIMON   *[Beat]* What?

JUSTIN   Die for my faith.

SIMON   Not on purpose.

JUSTIN   Not on purpose, no. But the minute we go out and proclaim the good news of Jesus and share all we own and help the poor and the orphans and widows, you *know* that someone is going to want to kill us.

SIMON   True. Okay, but –

[Simon is suddenly struck by another vision.]

SIMON   Hey, I've just had another vision.

JUSTIN   Really? I didn't have one. What was your vision?

SIMON   I think we should spread out from this town and tell *everyone* about Jesus.

JUSTIN   You mean, let *everyone* in to our... our... what should we call it?

SIMON   Church.

JUSTIN   That's a silly name. Where'd you come up with that?

SIMON   I don't know. It just popped into my head.

JUSTIN   Anyway, you think we should let everyone into our church?

SIMON   As long as they repent and are baptised, sure.

JUSTIN   I'd feel better about it if I had had the same vision...

SIMON   I'm telling you, it's what God wants us to do.

JUSTIN   Well... okay. Go ahead.

SIMON   *[Goes over to his desk]* I'll make a note of that. *[Writes furiously]* Several, in fact.

JUSTIN   We just got started and you're already writing memos?

SIMON   *Letters.* I'm writing *letters.*

JUSTIN   *[He goes to his desk]* Come to think of it, we better write down everything Jesus said and did while it's fresh in our minds. That way the whole – uh, *church* – will know what happened. *[He scribbles quickly]*

SIMON   Good idea. If we don't get it written down, then people will get confused. Let's face it: the great oral tradition is reliable, but it's nothing like the written word.

JUSTIN   Years from now people will thank us.

SIMON   If we're going to reach everyone, then the stories about Jesus should be tailored for specific readers – for maximum effectiveness.

JUSTIN   What do you mean?

SIMON   Well… we should do one for our own people, one for the pagans, one for the more learned philosophers in the world, and one that's all-inclusive.

JUSTIN   All-inclusive? How do we do that?

SIMON   Use more poetic terms like 'light', and 'love' and things like that. Ask John, he'll know how to do it.

JUSTIN   Right.

SIMON   You should also –

JUSTIN   Wait a minute. Who put *you* in charge?

SIMON   What?

JUSTIN   You're telling me to do all these things. I don't remember anybody saying you were the boss.

SIMON   It was just an idea. *[Beat]* Besides, I saw him first.

JUSTIN   What do you mean?

SIMON   I met Jesus before the rest of you. I've known him longer. And I may be wrong, but I think he liked me best of all.

JUSTIN   Now, hold on there –

SIMON   I'm also older and have more experience. So I should be in charge. *[Beat, pretending as if he had a vision]* I just had another vision!

JUSTIN   You did not.

SIMON   I did! God wants me to be in charge!

JUSTIN   Cut it out.

SIMON   He does!

JUSTIN   You're making this up.

SIMON   I'm serious. Do *you* want to be in charge?

JUSTIN   Not really. I thought we could be... democratic.

SIMON   You're joking. That'll never work with a new movement like ours. We need a... a *hierarchy*...

JUSTIN   A what?

SIMON   Well, let's say hypothetically that I'm the boss, what I'll need are assistants to help make decisions.

JUSTIN   What kind of assistants?

SIMON   I'll call them... uh... things like Bishops and Presbyters and Deacons and Elders.

JUSTIN　Where are you getting these names?

SIMON　They keep popping into my head. Anyway, these men will be like Jesus and the disciples were – the boss and his lieutenants – to help to make sure that the churches will be run properly.

JUSTIN　*Churches?* I thought *we're* the church?

SIMON　We're the mystical body of believers called the Church – with a capital 'C'. I'm talking about churches with a little 'c' which are the buildings we'll meet in.

JUSTIN　Hold on. We're meeting in people's homes now. You want to actually *call them* churches and get us all killed?

SIMON　Calm down. This persecution against us won't last forever. Even now the government is falling apart. As things relax, we'll take over and build proper places of worship – big, vast buildings that will glorify God. We'll call them *cathedrals*.

JUSTIN　You have quite an imagination.

SIMON　This is basic stuff. So, anyway, people will come to the churches and worship and pray and hear preaching. *[Beat, another thought]* But we have to make sure all the churches are preaching the same thing. We need to work out some basic ideologies.

JUSTIN　We sure do. People are already making a mess out of the books and letters we're circulating.

SIMON　How so?

JUSTIN　Some of them are saying that Jesus isn't God... and others are saying that he was half-man and half-God, but not totally both... and others say that he was sort of man, but not really, and sort of God, but not entirely and... well, it's a mess.

SIMON   Any ideas of what to do about it?

JUSTIN   I think we need to formally pull together our books and letters so that we're all reading and understanding the same thing.

SIMON   Okay...

JUSTIN   The first part of it will contain the traditional writings of our people.

SIMON   The Old Testament – right.

JUSTIN   The second part of it will contain the new books and letters that we've been circulating since Jesus left.

SIMON   The New Testament. Good, very good. We'll call the whole thing the Holy Book – or the Bible.

JUSTIN   You really are a clever fellow. But don't you think we'll need more?

SIMON   More?

JUSTIN   People aren't going to read the whole thing in a day. We need to summarise what we believe so that people will understand quickly and concisely.

SIMON   Oh! You mean a *creed* of some sort.

JUSTIN   Sure.

SIMON   *[Hands him some papers]* I just happen to have a couple written up already.

JUSTIN   *[Looks over the pages]* 'I believe in God the Father Almighty, maker of heaven and earth...'

SIMON   That first one I called the Apostles' Creed. That

second one is the Nicene Creed. I think they'll do the job.

JUSTIN   Looks good to me. Simple declarations of belief. They'll help a lot. *[Moves to desk]* But there are a few other things...

SIMON   Like what?

JUSTIN   *[Sorts through papers]* Inquiries about various subjects. They're what I call the 'If this, then that' letters. I don't know how to answer them.

SIMON   Let's have a go and see what we can come up with.

JUSTIN   Here's one – this is from the provinces – the writer begins 'Dear Abbey...' *[Beat]* Why do you suppose they wrote that?

SIMON   Because of where we're staying. I call this place an 'abbey'.

JUSTIN   You really have to keep me informed when you come up with new names like that.

SIMON   Go on.

JUSTIN   'Dear Abbey... If Jesus said at the last supper that the bread was his body and the wine was his blood, then weren't they *literally* his body and blood?'

SIMON   I think so. Do you think so?

JUSTIN   Sounds good to me.

SIMON   What else?

JUSTIN   *[Next letter]* 'Dear Abbey... If Jesus is God and Mary was the mother of Jesus, then doesn't that make her the Mother of God?'

SIMON   Makes sense to me.

JUSTIN   So it's all right?

SIMON   Sure. What else?

JUSTIN   'Dear Abbey... If the first believers were as important as we say, then shouldn't we give them special status to show how much we respect and admire them?'

SIMON   Sounds like a good idea. *[Goes to his desk to make a note]* Let's call them *saints*. God's representatives on earth... *[Scribbles]* only they're now in heaven.

JUSTIN   Wait a minute... If they were God's representatives on earth, but they're now alive in heaven, then they're still God's representatives, right?

SIMON   Sure.

JUSTIN   Except, now that they're in heaven, they're like *our* representatives, too, because they were human and understand how we fell, right?

SIMON   I suppose.

JUSTIN   So maybe we could *talk* to them and tell them what we're thinking and what we need and then they could put in a good word for us with God.

SIMON   But if you're going to think about it that way, then you might as well say that... that we should pray to Mary because, as the Mother of Jesus, she could help us out, too.

JUSTIN   Yeah!

SIMON   *[Thinks about it a second]* Okay. *[Beat, writes it down]* See? All we have to do is think this stuff through and we'll come up with all kinds of good ideas.

JUSTIN   You realise, of course, that *we're* God's representatives on earth, too...

SIMON   Not exactly.

JUSTIN   We're not?

SIMON   Well, we *are* – but it's a hierarchy – like I said... See, I'm the boss, so that makes me *more* of his representative than the people under me. And *they're* more of his representatives than the people under *them*... and on down the line until we get to the priests.

JUSTIN   Priests.

SIMON   The Vicars who run the churches. Just another word I made up. *[Beat]* It's a delegation of responsibilities, a distribution of power. All the best companies are run that way.

JUSTIN   I get it. *[Beat, picks up a letter]* But there's a group that doesn't.

SIMON   Doesn't get what?

JUSTIN   The idea that you should be the boss.

SIMON   The nerve.

JUSTIN   They say if you don't back off, they're going to split away.

SIMON   Let them split off then – see where it gets them.

JUSTIN   If you say so.

SIMON   Some people are so... so *orthodox* in their thinking. Well, it's their loss. They're going to miss a great time.

JUSTIN   Is something going on that I don't know about?

SIMON   Power, my friend. We're no longer a cultish little group from the Middle East. We have influence in politics, with Kings and Queens, with the fate of the nations. Our world is now a *Christian* world – with the church at the centre.

JUSTIN   Isn't that dangerous? You know what power does to people.

SIMON   What?

JUSTIN   It corrupts them.

SIMON   Jesus didn't say that.

JUSTIN   He said something *like* it.

SIMON   No, he didn't.

JUSTIN   I can't quote chapter and verse, but I'm sure he did.

SIMON   I'm sorry, but I can't help but think that this is all God's doing. Why put us in a position of power and influence unless it was part of his plan?

JUSTIN   *[Uneasily]* Well... that *may* be true.

SIMON   On to other things. I've been thinking about this whole business of our being God's representatives on earth – like the first believers, the saints – and it occurred to me that it might be up to us to determine whether people are saved or not.

JUSTIN   What?

SIMON   Think it through. We're part of the succession of leaders that goes all the way back to the first believers – the ones who Jesus gave the keys to the kingdom, right?

JUSTIN   Yeah...

SIMON   And people come to us for baptism and

confirmation and confession and everything else that has to do with their souls because the church is their gateway to God and heaven, right?

JUSTIN   Yeah...

SIMON   And if we *don't* let them into church, then their souls are in jeopardy, right?

JUSTIN   Yeah...

SIMON   Then that means that we actually determine whether people are saved or not.

JUSTIN   When you put it that way, then yeah, I suppose so. What about it?

SIMON   Well, there are some really good people who've made some mistakes – you know, sinned and all that. Good people who are influential and have a lot of money.

JUSTIN   So?

SIMON   It seems like a waste to have them ousted from the church just because of a few petty things like... adultery or depravity or embezzling or causing a few wars.

JUSTIN   What's your point?

SIMON   I want to let them back into the church.

JUSTIN   Because they repented.

SIMON   Well, technically, yes – but mostly because they're willing to give the church a lot of money to let them back in.

JUSTIN   Bribes?

SIMON   Don't be so crass. Not bribes. I was thinking of calling them... *indulgences.*

JUSTIN Why?

SIMON Because we're indulging them in their desire to come back to the church – heck, I don't know.

JUSTIN Heck?

SIMON Another word I made up. You didn't want me to say *hell*, did you?

JUSTIN No. *[Beat]* So let me get this straight: people who have been put out of the church as a punishment for their sinful misconduct can come back in to the church if they're willing to pay for it?

SIMON Yeah – that's the idea.

JUSTIN I don't like it.

SIMON What do you mean you don't like it?

JUSTIN I don't like it. I'm against it.

SIMON You can't be against it.

JUSTIN But I am. There's nothing in any of our papers, books and letters that allows for such a thing.

SIMON Well, I'm the boss and I say we can do it.

JUSTIN And I'm saying that, boss or not, you can't. It's wrong.

SIMON Says who?

JUSTIN Says the Bible.

SIMON What if I say that I supersede what the Bible has to say?

JUSTIN Then I say you're wrong and I won't listen to you.

SIMON Then I won't let you in my church.

JUSTIN   *Your* church? It isn't *your* church.

SIMON   It sure is. It was handed down to me over the generations.

JUSTIN   And I say it's handed down to those who have faith like the first believers had faith, those who hold to the Bible – not your ideas and traditions.

SIMON   My ideas and traditions came *before* the Bible, don't forget.

JUSTIN   But once God gave us the Bible, it became the standard by which your ideas and traditions are measured.

SIMON   Nonsense. You better straighten up or I'll throw you out.

JUSTIN   You can't throw me out! If you don't straighten up, I'll leave!

SIMON   I have nothing more to say to you. *[Goes to his desk]*

JUSTIN   Fine. I'll worship on my own, then. *[Goes to his desk]*

SIMON   Heretic.

JUSTIN   Papist.

SIMON   What?

JUSTIN   It's a word I just made up. See? You're not the only one who can make words up.

SIMON   But your words don't count like mine do.

JUSTIN   They count all right. *[Looks through his papers]* Let's see… the first thing I'm going to get rid of is… hmmm… this nonsense about the bread and wine in communion being the literal body and blood of Jesus. No more. It's something else. Something harder to explain. It's a mystery – something that become *like* the body and blood. *[Tears up paper]* There goes your tradition.

SIMON   Ha. Well *two* can play at that game. I don't think the bread and wine are a mystery at all. I think they're simply a *memorial* – symbols to remember Jesus by. *[Tears up paper]*

JUSTIN   *[Picks up paper]* You say God speaks only through his representatives on earth? Well, *I* say every person of faith has direct access to God through Christ. It's a matter of free will. *[Tears up paper]*

SIMON   *[Picks up paper]* You say that Man has free will, I say we are predestined by God to believe or not believe. God is sovereign! *[Tears up paper]*

JUSTIN   Oh yeah? *[Picks up paper]* Then if God is sovereign, then his Spirit is constantly at work in our lives and we don't need you or *anyone* to tell us what to do. His revelation is continual! *[Tears up paper]*

SIMON   *[Picks up paper]* Continual? Then his Spirit works in our hearts and we don't even need the *church* except as a means of corporate worship and fellowship. It's every man for himself! *[Tears up the paper, beat]* I think I need to be re-baptised, just to wash those old traditions off of my skin.

JUSTIN   Fine – you do that. Go dunk yourself. I don't have to be re-baptised to be a Christian. Not as long as I'm in line with the revelation of the Bible, God's living word, then I'm all right!

SIMON   You're only all right if God says you're all right.

JUSTIN   But God says I'm all right thanks to his *grace*.

SIMON   But his grace is only made clear by our *works*.
Do you take care of the poor? Do you dress in
an opulent manner? Do you drink excessively?
Do you read anything other than scriptures?

JUSTIN   Let's be reasonable…

SIMON   *You* be reasonable, I'm going to live *by faith*.
[Kneels] I throw myself humbly before God.

JUSTIN   You should throw yourself under a moving cart.
I'm not impressed by your kneeling. I'll stand
boldly like a son of my father and raise my
hands! *[He raises his hands]*

SIMON   It's nothing but show. God knows your heart.

JUSTIN   And *I* know *your* heart. Give up your false
religion.

SIMON   Mine is the true religion. Yours is just a fad.

JUSTIN   We'll see who lasts.

SIMON   We sure will.

JUSTIN   You should straighten up.

SIMON   *You* straighten up.

SIMON & JUSTIN TOGETHER
Get out or get killed!

[Suddenly Justin has a vision.]

JUSTIN   Wait! I just had a vision!

SIMON   What?

JUSTIN   I said I just had a vision.

SIMON   I can't understand a word you're saying.

JUSTIN   Are you deaf?

SIMON   What? Quit speaking gibberish and say what
          you have to say in English.

JUSTIN   This is amazing. *[Begins to dance around]* I feel
          wonderful... light-hearted... filled with love
          and... this must've been what it was like for the
          first believers at Pentecost! I'm filled with the
          Spirit of God! This is *great*!

SIMON   Great? What's great?

JUSTIN   Oh – you can understand me now?

SIMON   Yeah – once you stopped all that mumbo-
          jumbo. Why are you dancing around?

JUSTIN   I... I had a vision and I've been filled with the
          Spirit of God!

SIMON   No way.

JUSTIN   What are you talking about? I *did*!

SIMON   Well, *I* didn't have a vision, so yours must not
          be a real vision. What did you have for dinner
          last night?

JUSTIN   I'm telling you, I had a vision and felt the Spirit
          of God pour through me. That's why you didn't
          understand what I was saying. It's amazing.
          Everyone should experience this! It makes me
          want to go out and... and *heal* someone. *[Moves
          towards Simon]*

SIMON   Keep your hands to yourself.

JUSTIN   Don't you trust me?

SIMON   No. Your so-called vision was a mistake.

JUSTIN   It wasn't a mistake. Just because you didn't
          have one doesn't mean it wasn't real. Can I
          help it that I'm closer to God than you are?

SIMON   I resent that.

JUSTIN   In fact, it makes me wonder what's wrong with
         you.

SIMON   Wrong with *me*?

JUSTIN   Why didn't you see the vision? Why aren't you
         experiencing what I'm experiencing? Maybe
         you aren't saved.

SIMON   *What?*

JUSTIN   If you were truly saved, then you'd have the
         same kind of experience as I'm having.

SIMON   I think your experience is of the devil.

JUSTIN   And I think you're out of God's will.

SIMON   Oh yeah? And I think you're out of God's will
         because you're doing something that he didn't
         okay.

JUSTIN   It's in the Bible.

SIMON   Not the way you're doing it. Besides, times have
         changed. We know so much more now than we
         did before. Science and technology are leading
         us into new areas.

JUSTIN   You can keep your science and technology. I
         believe in the Bible.

SIMON   I believe in the Bible, too. Metaphorically
         speaking.

JUSTIN   Liberal!

SIMON   Fundamentalist!

JUSTIN   You're bowing to the whims of the age!

SIMON   And you're clinging to the past!

JUSTIN   I won't listen to you.

SIMON   You're just being stubborn. There's a rational explanation if you'll only open your eyes...

JUSTIN   God's word stands true no matter what you say.

SIMON   What good is his word if it isn't *relevant*? Hmm? God is love – so let's stop all the fighting.

JUSTIN   Fighting is all right, so long as the cause is just.

SIMON   Thou shalt not kill.

JUSTIN   Thou shalt not commit adultery.

SIMON   Love is free. Your institutions are dead. Jesus could come back any second, man. Do you think he'll care whether you're in a big old building or not? *[Taps heart]* The church is in *here*, not in your buildings and meetings and traditions. It's the Bible and *us*.

JUSTIN   *[Pause/beat]* That sounds familiar.

SIMON   What does?

JUSTIN   What you just said. I think someone has said it before.

SIMON   They couldn't have, because I just said it for the first time.

JUSTIN   Don't you think that... that... we're *not* the first?

SIMON   Of course we're not the first. There was the first-century church.

JUSTIN   I mean since then.

SIMON   There isn't any 'since then'. It was the first-century church and the Bible – and then *us*. Everything in between is irrelevant. Nobody cares anyway. We have to reach people right where they are if we're going to win them to Christ.

JUSTIN   I agree. *[Goes to desk]* And I've worked out four simple steps to get them there... all in this little pamphlet.

SIMON   You must be joking. Pamphlets! We have to think bigger than that.

JUSTIN   Bigger?

SIMON   Radio... television... we'll air our church services so people can hear me preach.

JUSTIN   Church? Look, statistics show that the average person doesn't go near anything resembling church any more. Its traditions and ideas are outmoded.

SIMON   What are you saying?

JUSTIN   We have to seek out the lost and create services that will make them feel comfortable. We need our churches to be completely *unlike* churches so they'll come in. *[Hands some pages to Simon]* Have a look at this format... See? Simple choruses, a selection of contemporary songs, and oh – I've got some drama sketches you can do, too.

SIMON   This seems really watered down. I mean, Christianity has lost its influence in our society and we've got to get it back.

JUSTIN   How?

SIMON   By being firm – by standing for the truth.

JUSTIN   But how do we communicate that truth?

SIMON   By negative reinforcement. We have to boycott and protest against anyone who doesn't agree with our truth, that's how! It's the only way to turn the tide of our decadent world.

JUSTIN   That's okay for society, but I'm worried about the average Christian out there. Our marketing research shows that Christians have a lot of personal problems and we have to help them somehow.

SIMON   For example?

JUSTIN   First, we need to create specific Bibles for every specific need we can think of.

SIMON   Victims of abuse, victims of addictions, victims of victims...

JUSTIN   Vegetarians, animal rights, people who've been born with six fingers...

SIMON   There's a gender consideration, too.

JUSTIN   True. I'm going to create a series of magazines to deal with women.

SIMON   I think I'll start a series of meetings for men. Maybe we'll gather in large stadiums.

JUSTIN   Promise?

SIMON   Sure.

JUSTIN   It's a new day. We'll let everyone in.

SIMON   Well, not *everyone*.

JUSTIN   Why not?

SIMON   We have to draw lines – have standards and parameters –

JUSTIN   Meaning what? We want to be inclusive, don't we?

SIMON   Sure. Inclusive to those who believe in the Bible the way we believe in it.

JUSTIN   The Bible says that God is love – he loves us regardless of what we think of the Bible.

SIMON   Sin is still sin. Surely we can't let people in who persist in sinning.

JUSTIN   And you're a bigoted hate-monger to think that way.

SIMON   And you're a spineless wimp who won't stand up for what's right, what's *biblical*.

JUSTIN   It depends on how you interpret it. What's right for you may not be right for me. It's subjective.

SIMON   Says who?

JUSTIN   Says me.

SIMON   But does *God* say so?

JUSTIN   Who are you to say whether he says so or not? That's between me and him. It has nothing to do with you.

SIMON   Oh.

JUSTIN   No retort? No response?

SIMON   I'm sure there's an answer but… I'm feeling awfully tired now.

JUSTIN   I'm getting a little worn down myself.

SIMON   How long has it been?

JUSTIN   Two thousand years.

SIMON   Sometimes it seems like yesterday.

JUSTIN   And sometimes it seems like two thousand years. Uh... where do we go from here?

SIMON   Seems like the only way to survive is to get together. Forget the peripherals and the nit-picking. We need to get back to the basics of our core faith.

JUSTIN   Yeah. Good idea.

SIMON   You have your people ring my people and we'll give it a try.

JUSTIN   Okay. One of these days.

[Suddenly they both perk up as if they've been given a vision.]

SIMON   I think I had a vision!

JUSTIN   Me, too!

[Whatever it was seems to have passed. They relax.]

SIMON   No, I suppose not.

JUSTIN   My mistake.

SIMON   Too bad. I could've used one.

JUSTIN   Same here.

SIMON   I guess I'll see you around.

JUSTIN   Yeah... see you.

[They move to exit on opposite sides. Justin stops at the edge.]

JUSTIN   You know...

[Simon stops and turns to him.]

SIMON   What?

JUSTIN   I've got this feeling that there's something we're supposed to do.

SIMON   Me, too. But I can't imagine what it is…

JUSTIN   *[Shrugs]* Same here.

SIMON   Bye. *[He exits]*

JUSTIN   Goodbye. *[He exits]*

Blackout. [Curtain.]

52 Quick Sketches – another great drama book by Paul McCusker

- **■** *A minute to rehearse*
- **■** *A minute to perform*
- **■** *Relevant themes and issues*
- **■** *Ideal for sermon illustrations, drama groups, schools and discussion groups*

Themes include: AIDS, singleness, church splits, dating unbelievers, evangelism, family tensions, lateness, midlife crisis, ordination of women, lust, guilt and many more.

---

52 Quick Sketches
Paul McCusker
ISBN 1 85424 527 9

Available from your local Christian Bookshop.
In case of difficulty contact Monarch Books,
Concorde House, Grenville Place, Mill Hill, London NW7 3SA.

MONARCH
BOOKS